FROM POST TO POST

First published in 2006 by
CURRACH PRESS
55A Spruce Avenue, Stillorgan Industrial Park, Blackrock, Co. Dublin

www.currach.ie

1 3 5 4 2

Cover by Bluett
Origination by Currach Press
Printed by ColourBooks Baldoyle Industrial Estate Dublin 13

ISBN: 1-85607-936-8

FROM POST TO POST

TONY BEATTY

CURRACH
PRESS

To my wife Breda and our children, Catherine, Claire and Ian
and in memory of our son Paul Anthony

CONTENTS

FOREWORD

Having crossed paths with Tony Beatty for so many years I feel privileged to pen the foreword for a book which not only epitomises his real journey through life but succeeds in highlighting a distinguished and colourful career. Here is a man who has overcome adversity to emerge with a high degree of courage and determination, and a refusal to accept what many would see as the inevitable.

Tony Beatty has created a book which can be seen as a source of inspiration and hope as well as being both humorous and reflective. It tells the story of someone born and reared in a rural village in Waterford, one who has climbed the heights of success through sheer grit and determination. Those who resort to the book in search of inspiration and those who are moved to read it through simple curiosity will find its contents both absorbing and uplifting. The book begins with family life, featuring the comings and goings of a community that thrived on comradeship and trust. It follows the footsteps of a man who set out with a goal in mind and succeeded in achieving this goal. It tells of a man who reached the sublime heights of his profession, one who eventually was forced to give way to an illness that robbed him of achieving even greater recognition, especially on the field of sport. Here, his engagement in golf, soccer and Gaelic football was curtailed at an age when higher honours were there for the taking.

Tony Beatty's achievements were many. Having reached the top in his accountancy profession, he turned his attention towards the formation of a newspaper, aimed principally at the Irish community in Britain. And, thanks to his foresight, this newspaper enjoys a wide readership in all parts of Britain today. As testimony to his skills as a fundraiser, he has been widely acclaimed by Church and state leaders for his charitable work, going so far as to rescue a number of organisations from financial oblivion. Certainly Tony Beatty has led a colourful and full life, despite suffering from an illness which may have restricted his movements, but not his ambitions.

This book is unique in that nothing of its kind has previously been attempted. It is factual, honest and full of humour. From the opening chapter to the final full stop it embraces a richness and depth that bring home to the reader that here is someone who has refused to accept adversity in his efforts to point the way to others.

My best wishes are extended to Tony Beatty for his courage in writing a book that is certain to give the same pleasure to other readers as it did to me.

Jerry Daly

(I was very sad to hear of the death of Jerry Daly on 25 March 2006. He was a true Kerry gentleman. May he rest in peace.

Tony Beatty)

I

EARLY YEARS

Thursday 26 September 1935 was special for the Beatty family. Yes, I arrived that day. The other newsworthy matters for that period are shown in *The Birthday Times* of that date. I wonder, but never heard, if my dad backed 'Reynoldstown', the winner of the 1935 Grand National. Of course there were many other interesting items shown: the average annual income was £235; a gallon of petrol cost 1s/6d (7.5p in today's money) a three bedroom house £750. Yet the most important piece of news, my birth, is missing.

I was born in my grandmother's house at 1 Millbrook Terrace, Kilmacthomas, County Waterford, and as was normal at that time I was brought to the church the next day to be baptised. My full name is Bernard Anthony but I was to be known as Tony. My godmother was Mary Bushell, a neighbour and friend of my mother. I do not know much about this lady. In fact I cannot remember any meetings or discussions with her although some may have occurred in my very early days. My godfather was a postman, a friend of my father. His name was Frank Cashin. At the celebration after the baptism, Frank, who was one of the thousands of Irish lads involved with the British Army in the First World War (1914–18) said, 'You know that I have many souvenirs of the war and that I have no sons. Therefore I have decided I will

give them all to young Tony when he is old enough to understand.'
My dad replied, 'I know how much those items mean to you,
Frank, so all I can do is to say, on behalf of Tony, thank you.'

My grandmother's house was nice and cosy, with three
bedrooms, a living room/kitchen and a scullery. The living room
had a black range around which everyone sat – the wireless was
also in that room. The scullery, which was very cold in the winter,
was off this room. During this time lighting was by paraffin
lamps and candles and the toilet was at the bottom of the garden.
It was, I suppose, about three years before I found out (vaguely)
what was going on. I have vague memories of my mother and
father during this time but, going back a long, long way, I can
remember my grandmother, Catherine. Yes, I can recall this very
friendly lady. She had white hair, tied in a bun, always wore black
clothes and was proud of her appearance. Her dresses were just
below mid-calf length and she wore black stockings and shoes.
When the local dance hall was in use she always worked there and
I can recall her bringing home lots of coloured hats and ribbons
– wonderful things to a young child!

My sister, Mary, arrived on 15 July 1937. This was, of course,
very special and exciting for the family. A few months after
her birth, Mary, in her pram, and myself were taken for regular
walks around the village and the local roads by my mother. My
memories of those walks and talks are now virtually non-existent.
I can now remember only what I was told about later.

There was a big factory in our village – Flahavan's. Their most
famous product is porridge. So long as I can remember every
morning at home until I went to England it was porridge with
which I started every day. Most times it had milk and sugar added,
but then in the later years cream took the place of milk. Not good
for those with a weight problem – but delicious!

Saturday evening was the time for baths. I was bathed by my
mother for the first few years of my life; it was lovely getting a

bath in front of the range. My uncles usually came in during the operation and particularly my uncle Tommy used to make the comment to my mother (his sister: 'Don't forget, Mamie, it is my turn next for the bath.' My mother used to say, 'Go away, Tommy, you can see I'm busy.' So Tommy, after his tea, used to go out to his friends.

A few interesting things happened in 1939, all in September. We moved into a new council house – 9 St Anne's Terrace. I can vividly remember the move from my grandmother's house. My dad had arranged for a horse-drawn cart to take our possessions to the new place. I can remember the driver put me up on the front of the cart with him. That month too saw the birth of my second sister, Eileen, on 22 September.

I started school in October 1939. My name is on the register written up by Mother Aloysius. My mother accompanied me and then, after school each day, she called to take me home. This lasted for some months until she decided that I could go on my own. The school was organised as follows: the junior infants were at one end of the classroom, the senior infants at the other end with an open fire in between them around which stood in winter the children's bottles of milk or cocoa with the corks or caps loosened to prevent a minor explosion which could also cause a major distraction. When there were two rows of bottles, at mid-morning the outside row was changed to the inside and at ten minutes to lunchtime all the bottles were moved back so that our tiny hands could handle them safely. The sister in charge of the classes did all the changing, making sure that the bottles were now outside the high, strong, black, angular fireguard. My classmates and I ate sandwiches of home-made bread and butter or bread and jam. We always ate in a hurry; the faster we ate the more time we had for play. On wet days when we couldn't go out we went sliding up and down the convent entrance hall which always became damp when the weather changed.

I was getting very active in the early 1940s and made a good friend of classmate Mervyn Battye. His parents had a holiday home near the strand in Bonmahon. I was about seven years old when I was taken on my first-ever holiday. I had heard Mervyn's parents on a few occasions discuss their seaside holiday house at the strand. When my dad told me that I would be going on holiday there with the Battye family for seven days I was very excited and really looked forward to it. I was taken there in the Battye family car. Nothing like this had ever happened to me before. Being upset and missing my parents just did not enter my head. The first day was great. I spent a lot of time on the strand with my friends and when I got back to the house and had tea it was time for bed. I slept well and then got up early to start the second day. Getting out and about was great but on this day I really began to miss my mum, dad and family. The next day was interesting. I was taken for a journey to a number of local scenic places. However it became clear that missing my family was too important and it was agreed to take me home on the Thursday. I was so delighted to see my parents that I felt holidays in the future would have to be family holidays only. So that was my first holiday ended.

I can vaguely remember later that year being taken by my grandmother to two shops in the village that sold toys in December. It was a big treat. My grandmother also kept chickens and it was a big treat for the family to have chicken for Christmas dinner. I can remember them being killed and plucked.

When the war rationing started every house had to be careful and plan each week as though it was the last week. There was, of course, no white bread and even the brown bread was rationed. One loaf per head daily was allowed. The butter allowance was six ounces per person, tea a mere half an ounce and sugar six ounces each. Clothes were rationed, each person being given an allowance of coupons. Private cars were all off the road and only a small ration of petrol was allowed for hackneys. Paraffin oil was restricted to farmers for tractors. There was compulsory tillage for farmers. I understand that deals were done between families to ensure that each week all the rations were used. I can recall the 'black' bread. It was not nice but during the war years my parents always had enough food for the family. We took this for granted and did not realise at the time how hard it was for them. Times were tough but we survived.

My dad was in the Local Security Force (LSF). He had a dark-blue uniform which he wore each night when going out with colleagues to guard the area by walking out and confirming that everything was normal. My uncles, being younger than my father, belonged to the other organisation, the Local Defence Force (LDF). This group wore brown uniforms and were armed with rifles. Apart from marching in the streets, they did armed training in the local workhouse grounds. I used to be taken there to see them in action. The Irish army also used to send battalions to march and parade in the village. It was all very exciting for a young lad, seeing the army vehicles and the soldiers. At that time I was really enjoying life and certainly did not appreciate what a wonderful job my parents were doing.

I now gather a few words together to describe the condition of my parents as I remember them during those years. My mother Mary (known as Mamie to her friends) was always at home and prepared to listen and help where she could. She had the ability to make us feel very much part of the family and appreciated. She was naturally intelligent, a quiet unassuming person, a good listener and a very good manager. Her religion was very important to her. She and our father made sure that, as a family, we said the rosary every evening after tea and saw to it that we fulfilled all our religious obligations. My father, Bernard – known to everyone as Ben – was also a very good Christian. As a postman he helped anyone that he could, especially on his daily postal route. He called the doctor to the sick, the vet to sick animals, collected prescriptions from the chemist and talked to people with problems. He also collected bets from anyone who wanted to back a horse and brought the proceeds to them the next day if the horse won. He always helped us with homework. He was an avid reader, getting many books from the local library every week. He was an extremely methodical person and dealt promptly with any correspondence – always on the day he received it. Any business acumen that I have was inherited from both my parents. They were a good team and managed very well.

During the 1940s I can remember my father bringing me on the bar of his bicycle to hurling and football matches when the local teams were involved, particularly St Anne's, the Kilmacthomas junior hurling team, with their red shirts with one white stripe. As a result of those trips I began to find out about those sports and how they were played. Because my father was a postman it meant steady pay and, as a result, we always had regular meals. His income meant that he could support his family. There was always enough to feed and clothe us, pay the rent and household expenses. Perhaps there was not a lot left over for luxuries but then, at Christmas, he used to get lots of 'Christmas boxes', which meant that we always had a plentiful Christmas.

I found out that there was a very special visitor with gifts for 'good children' at Christmas – Santa Claus or, as we knew him, 'Daddy Christmas'. The method was for us to write to him and tell him what we wanted. Before we were able to write, our parents wrote the letters for us and we posted them in the fireplace and watched the paper burning and going up the chimney. It was a mystery to me that he always brought the presents we wanted, plus one or two more that we didn't ask for – magical times.

The first time that I became vaguely aware that I had an Uncle Jack (my father's brother) was in March 1939, when he visited our home in Kilmacthomas, between voyages. That was when I found out that he was a merchant sailor. A while later when my dad took me out for a walk I talked to him about my uncle. He told me, 'Your uncle has travelled all over the world on voyages and when he met you on his last visit he told me that, when you are old enough to understand, he will tell you a few stories.' From that point onwards he became my hero.

He next called to meet us a few months later and, of course, I looked forward to his stories. Before he asked me to sit down I heard him talking to my dad, 'You know, Ben, that there is a lot of trouble in Europe. What do you think?'

Dad replied, 'It is like the First World War again. I can't see things any different. What will you do, Jack?'

He answered, 'The sea is in my blood, Ben. I have no other training. I will stay on ships and I hope that, as those ships are not fighters, we might get through safely.'

Dad replied, 'All I can say is – be careful.'

Jack said then, 'When I get on to a ship I will let you have the details. If the war starts I just don't know whether I will be involved. Tell Tony that I will talk to him when I next come here.'

Then on an early September Sunday I got home from Mass with my mum. Before lunchtime I knew that something big was going on. Of course I had no idea of the enormity of what was unfolding. Some neighbours, who did not have wirelesses, came to my grandmother's home. The news appeared to be very serious. Later on my dad told me what it was – the announcement that the Second World War had started. All the adults were very concerned. What would happen? Would we be involved? The locals, many of whom recalled what happened in the First World War, were upset and frightened. But for me I could only see a lot of excitement, including what I could remember about my Uncle Jack. He was in touch with my dad and told him that he was now fixed up on a ship going to America on a voyage which should keep him away from fighting for a spell. He also gave the following information about the trip:

The ship is called *Langleeford*. I have been a crew member on it a few times in the past and always enjoyed those trips. I have a bit of a holiday before the voyage starts. Here is the programme: she arrived in Cardiff on 3 November 1939, and was in dry dock under repair until 19 December. That was where I was to book in for the sailing on 21 December to Providence, Boston. But, as the saying goes – the best laid plans of mice and men gang aft agley. Yes, I missed the train from Dungarvan to Dublin. So when I finally got there and caught the connection to Wales I am afraid that I was too late for the sailing. I returned to Dungarvan and took an unexpected further holiday. The ship arrived at Providence on 13 January 1940 and reached Boston on the twentieth. She sailed on 25 January, arrived at Halifax on 27 January and sailed from there on 31 January to Tyneside in England. Whilst on that voyage the *Langleeford* was sunk by a German submarine on 14 February 1940. Four of her crew of 34 were lost.

On this enforced holiday after Christmas he visited us again. This time he fulfilled his promise to sit down with me. His stories were exciting and he gave me a few accounts of where he had been on his voyages: Montreal, Canada, Rotterdam, Holland, Sydney, New South Wales, the Black Sea, the Mediterranean, Central America, South America, Russia. This is just a short list of some of the places he went to. There is not enough space to document all his voyages. He became a crew member of the Irish

Shipping Company's boat, the *Irish Elm*, and later joined the local Dungarvan ship, the *Lady Belle*. This was mainly operating between Dungarvan and Britain. On one of his voyages, on 26 March 1941, the *Lady Belle* was attacked from the air by a German bomber while she was on a voyage from Dungarvan to Cardiff to collect a cargo of coal for her owners, the local firm of A. Moloney and Sons. It happened when she was ten miles south-east of the Smalls at the entrance to the Bristol Channel.

On the day of the attack he was captained by Captain O'Donoghue of Dungarvan. The following is an extract from his official log:

> A small plane approached from the south and dropped a bomb which parted the starboard anchor's cable, went through the forecastle head and ship's side in forecastle. The plane again attacked the vessel which was unarmed and what appeared to be a cannon shell took away the fore and port side of the wheel house, together with the compass. He then released two bombs which fell wide, one port and one starboard side. The pilot of the bomber brought his aircraft down to an altitude of 40ft, within a 30ft range and shelled the steamer with machine-gun fire, doing considerable damage to the deck fittings, masts, ship's side, upper works, also bursting deck steam pipes.

Despite extensive damage the *Lady Belle* made for Milford Haven under her own power; *all* the crew members escaped injury. The ship was 140ft in length and had a beam of 23ft 9ins. She carried a cargo of 339 tons. She was a well-known visitor to such ports as Swansea, Cork, Cardiff, Waterford and Liverpool. During her seagoing career most of her voyages were uneventful, but on 6

August 1935, while on a passage from Birkenhead to Baltimore with a cargo of coal, she was in a collision with another ship, the SS *San Adolfo*, happily with no loss of life.

Uncle Jack's last period as a sailor was with the Irish Shipping Company, mainly on the *Elm*. He retired in June 1951. I met him for the last time on a trip home from Dungarvan in March 1955. We had a very enjoyable chat. He died on 5 March, 1962. As a young boy I always found his stories magical. He will always be one of my heroes.

2

SCHOOLDAYS

Wages in the early 1940s were very low and, of course, treats were few and far between. As a result, First Holy Communion and Confirmation were simply never-to-be forgotten occasions. I made my First Confession in a confession box at the back of the wooden church attached to the convent and a few steps away from a side door to the school. The box had two doors for the penitents and a half-door in between for the priest. Above the half-door was a curtain through which the priest could look out to make sure that everything was in order and to see if there were many more people to come. We, the children, were not afraid in the dark box because we had had several 'pretend' confessions with our teacher in the weeks beforehand. I talked to my uncle Tommy about what I should tell to the priest? We had a good talk. He emphasised that whatever else happens – 'just remember that you must always tell the truth in confession.' My mother took me to Hadden's shop in Dungarvan in mid-February 1943 to order a suit for the big day.

That day started for me with my mother on the bus from Kilmacthomas to Dungarvan. When we got there we walked from the bus stop to the shop. Nothing like this had ever happened for me before. My mam said, 'I know that you are excited about this but stay quiet and I will do all the talking in the shop.' We got to the shop. I tried on a couple of dark suits and finally a navy suit was bought plus a bright white shirt. I was, of course, delighted and at last everything was ready for my big day. All my friends had also gone to shops in different towns to do the same job but, obviously, not on the same day. I really enjoyed this day out with my mam. It was just another of the little jobs that had to be done before my very big day.

First Holy Communion morning was very special. The top seats were reserved on one side for the boys in full suits and rosettes and on the other side for the girls all in white carrying candles dressed with flowers. The parents occupied the remaining seats at the back and a special children's choir in the gallery sang hymns in keeping with the occasion. One of them ended 'All my life I will remember this my First Communion Day' and another 'I love my cross, I love my beads, each emblem of my faith.'

The mothers especially loved the hymns and many of them could be seen wiping away silent tears. The prayers before and after Holy Communion were recited out loud by us children. At the altar rails a nun stood behind each child while he or she received Holy Communion so there was no room for fear or panic. The ceremony was followed by breakfast in the cookery room in the school. We, the children, had taken no food since 12 o'clock midnight. The meagre but welcome menu consisted of tea, bread and butter and buns, after which each child was presented with rosary beads and a prayer book by the Reverend Mother. The convent garden, forbidden at all other times, was thrown open to the children on their First Holy Communion day and they could stay until their parents came to collect them. We ran up to the various flights of steps, two or three steps at time, rolled down the slopes of the terraces, jumped over the hedges, leapt across the flowerbeds, to the annoyance of Gerry the gardener who refrained from passing any comment on this our special day. To all the nuns in the convent, listening to the sounds of laughter and joy, it was as if the garden had come alive. Not so long after that, on 1 July 1944, the other boys and I were transferred to Currabaha Boys National School at the other end of the village My sister Patricia (Patsy) was born on 18 March 1944. So now our family was six.

One day in August 1943 my dad told me that he had a lovely surprise in store for me. He said to my mother, 'Mamie, I know that Tony has never met his grandfather so I will take him by train to Dungarvan. Last time I spoke to my father a couple of weeks ago he said that he would love to see Tony.'

The big day arrived and as I went with my father to the railway station I was very excited. The journey started and looking out the windows and hearing my dad's comments were great. My dad said, 'I am delighted to see you so happy, but there is another surprise – just wait and see.' A few minutes later the surprise started. The train went into a tunnel – in the townland called Durrow – between Kilmacthomas and Dungarvan. It was very dark and I had no idea what was going on. Then the train was through the tunnel and everything was light again. Relief! My dad smiled and said 'Did you enjoy it?'

I said, 'It was lovely when I knew what was happening but I am glad that it is over.'

When we got to Dungarvan we walked to my grandfather's house. He was a lovely man. It was the first time I had ever seen a man with a beard. It was very exciting. We went out with my granddad for a walk, when he pointed out many things that were new to me. When we got back to his home and had a meal I was tired. It was time to go to the railway station then and to get the train back home to Kilmacthomas. I remembered the tunnel to come and reminded my dad. He laughed. We got home and my mam saw how excited I was. My dad said that on his next holidays he would take me to my grandfather again. About twelve months later he did and I also enjoyed that. Those two days were the only times I ever met my grandfather. I never met my grandmother,

Ellen. I understand she was born in New York and she died in her mid-forties, many years before I was born.

In those days there were storytellers in each village. Their stories were hair-raising to people like me, to such an extent that at the time I believed in ghosts and banshees. The stories ('true' ghost stories) were normally told by old people sitting around the fire on a winter's night or by Paddy Barron in his cobbler's shop. We were warned to avoid all graveyards after dark. That was the time, we were told, when the dead walked. I can remember asking many people for explanations. Without exception, the answer was always vague and about what third parties saw. I never met anybody who had seen a ghost but I heard lots of stories about what other people saw. For young people this was very frightening. We would not walk out on any dark road alone at night, so in those times the streets were clear after dark. Occasionally, from the age of ten onwards, I went out on walks at night with friends, 'daring' the dark. When elders in the village heard that we had gone for a walk after dark we were told to watch out. To this day, I do not know what we should have watched out for, but there is no doubt that the environment was such that we were apprehensive of the period after dark. Remember that, at the time, the method of lighting in most houses was a paraffin lamp.

Glen Bog is a few miles from our Kilmacthomas village. In the 1940s it was normal for families to rent a piece of bog and from May onwards the work commenced. I can recall being taken to Glen Bog a few times on the bar of my father's bicycle. Before the turf-cutting, certain work had to be done to prepare the ground. The heather had to be burned off and the dry mossy undergrowth then had to be dug off and thrown away. It was then time to start cutting the turf with the *sleán*. The new turf sods then had to be set out to dry. A lot of the other places were being worked in the bog and now and then the workers would have a break for a drink and a smoke. The drinks were either milk or minerals and it was not strange to see some of the younger lads having a few 'drags' from their older friends' cigarettes. Very few of the workers had watches at that time so the finishing time was normally six o'clock which was the time the Angelus Bell tolled. Tools were downed and cleaned then until the next day.

Strangely I cannot remember any bad days in those 1940s' summers. I was taken to the bog in 1942, 1943 and 1944. On the last year I borrowed my Aunt Kathleen's bicycle and joined my father on his trips. Each year when the turf was ready to be taken home we got a horse and cart to bring it and I always got a lift in the cart.

During the Second World War I could not recall the pre-war years when there were such things as white bread, cocoa, biscuits and sweets. At the time, the bread I remember was called 'black' bread. I had heard of such things as bananas, oranges and other fruits but had never seen them. One day a man arrived in our village looking for my father. He was given instructions by somebody about how to get to our house. Anyway, he was an acquaintance from my father's hurling days. When I got home from school, my mother said she had a special treat for us. It was a box of cocoa. I had never tasted anything like it. It was really delicious, and my mother's words a 'special treat' were an understatement.

In accordance with the Irish tradition I was taken to the local parish church (in Newtown) and baptised the day after my birth. My godmother was Mary Bushell, a neighbour and acquaintance of my mother. I do not know much about this lady. In fact I cannot remember any discussions or meetings with her, although some must have taken place in my very early days. My godfather was a postman friend of my father. His name was Frank Cashin. I have many recollections of meetings with him. As a very young lad I found out that he was a veteran of the First World War. He was one of the thousands of Irish lads who joined the British army and fought in that war. He told me many stories about the things that happened on the battlefields. My memories are quite vague but I can remember his promise to give me a special souvenir in due course. One day, when I was seven years old, he met me and asked me to call to his house for the promised souvenir. I did and he gave me something very special – the helmet which he had worn throughout the war. He was right about this – to a young boy that was very special. Then over the next year or so, he passed on to me some badges and buttons from his uniform – also very exciting.

A rumour went around the village in the early 1940s that we would soon have a cinema where talking films would be shown. This did not mean a lot to me so I talked to my father about it. He told me that before the war he had seen some films in Waterford. He described how a story was told, like bringing a book to life. I could not really comprehend this; to a young lad it meant bringing something to life on the cinema screen. I was excited about it and really looked forward to it happening. Anyway, at last, in 1942, it became public news and the first show and date were announced. I went with my father. The cinema was packed. The very first film shown was a Western – *Destry Rides Again*. I found the whole thing absolutely fascinating. For the next few months my father took me regularly to the 'pictures'. At that stage I thought that I was becoming an expert. Each week when the programme was advertised I picked out what I thought would be the best story. Then, financed by my parents, I went to see at least one film a week over the next few years. It was like going to school. I learnt a lot there.

From the time I was born our house was lit by a big paraffin oil lamp and candles. There was no alternative to these and we used them as a matter of fact because nothing else was available to us. A local business produced lights on the village main street at night. Electric light was special and no doubt I must have thought many times during the 1940s about how good it would be if only we had it. Then in the late 1940s a rumour started in the village that some time in 1950 the ESB (Electricity Supply Board) would install electricity in the whole mid-Waterford area. Such rumours had started previously about various matters but they were never fulfilled. There were further rumours about the electricity but until the workmen arrived it was not possible to believe them. Eventually the workmen arrived and at last it was truly a matter of when. One had to live there to appreciate the new lights and to see people's reaction. For me to be able to read easily, even in bed, took a little time to get used to. It was like a gift from Father Christmas. Just getting home and pressing a switch on the wall to fill the room with light was very special. This was living. I never, ever expected to live in such luxury.

I can recall being told one day that there would be a very famous Irishman visiting the area. I had no idea who it was but then one morning I was told, 'Today's the day.' I stayed in the village and then finally at about midday a few cars (about three I think) moved up the street and stopped. There must have been about thirty or forty people together at the top of the street. The car door was opened and Eamon de Valera got out. He made a little speech, shook hands with everyone there – yes, I was in the queue and really felt good about shaking hands with such a famous person. He then went to a supporter's house, spent some time there and finally moved on.

A kind of miracle happened in our family house at St Anne's Terrace, Kilmacthomas, in May 1963. My parents, my brother John, my two sisters, Patsy and Kathleen and I lived there at that time. My mother did some washing that day and, as was usual, when she took the clothes in from the clothesline in the garden, she put them on the line over the range for airing. At bedtime the clothes were still airing. Everyone went to bed for the night. In the early hours a big bang was heard downstairs. The whole family woke up. My father ran down the stairs, opened the kitchen door and shouted upstairs, 'Come down fast. Fire!' Everyone ran down the stairs. The front door was open but the kitchen door was closed. He opened it and there were flames everywhere. It appeared that the fire started when sparks from the range hit the clothes. The noise also woke the neighbours and as the flames prevented access to the water tap in our house they did the necessary, bringing in bucket after bucket of water. The fire was finally brought under control and the situation could be examined.

Practically everything in the kitchen was destroyed – all the furniture burned beyond recognition. The paint on the walls and ceiling was totally destroyed. But all the pictures except one were still hanging up. The one on the floor was the Sacred Heart picture. Its cord was broken and the glass was scattered around the floor. It became clear on examination that the fire had spread to the curtains and burnt a line of wallpaper straight across to the cord of the Sacred Heart picture, which fell to the hard floor with a bang. That was the noise that woke my parents, whose bedroom was immediately above the kitchen. If it were not for that noise my father would not have come down the stairs, the whole house would have burned down and obviously none of our family would have survived. A miracle? Perhaps not, but unquestionably a piece of divine good luck.

For many years, with little or no work in Ireland, the emigration ship beckoned. In the late 1940s many people left for America. My uncle, Paty Power, was one of those. He worked as a labourer in a local mill but decided that there was more to life than that. He had relatives in Boston, he got in touch with them and they agreed to accept him as an emigrant. His mother, my grandmother, was very upset about this but finally accepted that he would soon be on his way. A flight was arranged at Rineanna (now Shannon) Airport for the last Sunday in August 1947. Before he left the traditional party was held. The house was full.

Many friends called in to wish him well and to have a drink with him. There was lots of music also and the session ended in the early hours of the morning. When the hackney car called for him the goodbyes finally ended and all the promises about regular postal contact were made. Then he was away and, like mothers all over Ireland at the time, his mother took some time to get over her loss.

As a young boy in my village I remember reading such comics as the *Dandy*, *Beano*, *Adventure*, *Wizard* and *Hotspur* and exchanging them with other boys. The most popular Christmas presents of those days were guns and caps, hurleys, balls, games such as Ludo, draughts, Snakes and Ladders and playing cards. We wore short trousers in our schooldays and suffered cuts and bruises from thorns, brambles and nettles going through the fields and woods. I remember playing handball up against the post office wall and playing hurling and football on the roads, with stones used as goals in the wintertime and clothes in the summertime. It was always a problem when the ball went over a wall into some neighbour's garden. Some neighbours cooperated when we knocked on their doors but with others we had to run into their gardens, get the ball back and run. When we played cowboys and Indians we used to split into teams. The Indians hid in the woods and the cowboys found them and took them prisoner. Many hours and days were spent on those recreations. There were many other pastimes, in the summertime particularly, when we used to go Glen Bog on one of the carts from the village. They were going to collect their turf. I also remember going with my father on a horse and cart to pick up wood that he had bought from a local farmer for our winter fuel. I remember going, when I was ten years of age or so, to pick potatoes. The wages were 3s/6d (17.5p) a day. There were plenty of takers at that price.

An enjoyable pastime for the men was pitch and toss. Particularly during the summer evenings a couple of 'schools' were in action in the village. Men used to queue up to get into their favourite 'school'. A target stone would be set up. Each player tossed two old pennies at the target. Before they started the amount to be contributed by each player to make up the prize would be agreed. Then whoever had the coin that fell nearest to the target would have the first toss for a win of the cash at stake. Each player tossed two pennies and the first one to get two heads won the lot. Then the whole process was repeated.

I was born left-handed. As a result, it came naturally to me to use my left hand and arm. My parents never, at any time, indicated that using my left hand was different from or opposite to what most people did. I attended the convent school from October 1939 until I was transferred to the local boys' national school at the age of eight, and I cannot recall being told by the teachers, who were nuns, that my left-handed way was anything other than normal. Then to the boys' school. I cannot recall any problems during my first year, in third class. The next year I was transferred to fourth class. The first few weeks into the year were no different from previous years. Then one day I was working on an English composition. The teacher used to go from desk to desk to see how we were getting on, carrying his cane around with him. We used to wonder why he did this, as I could not remember him ever using it on those visits. Anyway he reached my desk and checked what I was writing. No comments from him but then he smacked the back of my left hand, knocking my pen on to the floor. It really hurt. Before I could ask why, the teacher said, 'You must write with your right hand. Any time I catch you writing with your left hand from now on you can expect a similar wallop.'

Now the pressure was on me. I really tried writing with my right hand but I did not seem to be making much progress. One day at school I tried something on a page of writing but as a result I ended up with a further rap, across my right hand this time. I asked the teacher why, as I was writing with my right hand. He said I should look at my sheet. He had found me out. I wrote with my left hand until I saw the teacher going to the desks to examine our work. Looking at my sheet I realised that, as some writing was slanted to the left and some to the right, it was obvious that I had used both hands. I finally got the hang of this and by the time I was twelve years old I used my right side normally. Ironically, when my multiple sclerosis affected my right side, I had to revert to my left for writing. A strange world!

In the mid- and late-1940s, when popular horse race bets were a shilling each way and a half-crown (12.5p) to win, my father used to place his bets through an acquaintance going to either Dungarvan or Waterford on the daily bus. There was no betting shop in our village at that time. Every evening I would go to my grandmother's house and mark the winners on the day's newspapers for him. My trip to my her house was through the local Kiersey's field. Sometimes my friends were hurling in that field. It was tough to pass them without taking part but one evening I gave into the temptation. That particular day my father wanted the results from only one meeting and I thought 'easy'. I got very involved in the hurling and forgot all about the races. Some time later it entered my head. I asked one of the lads who had a watch for the time and thought 'I'm in trouble.' It was far too late to go to my granny's so the only thing I could do was take my pencil, mark six 'winners' and take the paper to my father, muttering some excuse about the delay. He didn't make a big thing about my being late, so my markings must have looked all right but I suffered that night with thoughts like, 'What will he think when he sees the paper tomorrow?' But it was too late to change things.

All day at school I worried about going home and facing my dad. In those days he finished work at about 5 p.m. so I was home from school a bit earlier than that. Anyway he came in and after a while said he wanted to talk to me. Here goes, I thought. He said that I had made a mistake on the paper markings the day before, to which I replied, 'What do you mean?' He said, 'Be more careful in future – you marked only five winners and in the other race the horse you marked finished second.' Relief! Of course I said sorry to him. Some time later when I told him what had actually happened we both had a good laugh about it.

3

EXTRA LESSONS

Since there was no secondary school in the Kilmacthomas area, a school inspector asked the Reverend Mother if some of the nuns would undertake to teach a few extra subjects even for half an hour in the evenings for a small fee. They taught French, algebra and geometry to boys and girls. Then Sr Teresa ventured to try shorthand, typewriting and bookkeeping. Personally I was doing well at school and felt quite confident. One evening the Reverend Mother arrived in the classroom with a new pupil (me). Sr Teresa called me aside after the lesson and told me that the Reverend Mother had advised her that no fees must be taken from me because I was from a poor family. For the record, when I first called to the classroom I was welcomed and introduced to the other pupils. I was given a Gregg shorthand book and shown the ancient L. G. Smith typewriter. I was also given a bookkeeping textbook and was shown how to do the first lesson. Next time we met, a week later, I was as far as the third lesson. This was my introduction to bookkeeping and I loved it. I had been told that it was complicated but if it was complicated I couldn't see where. I did not find any problems. Next time we met I was halfway through the book and way beyond the class. I was asked some questions to find out if I understood it. My response was what nowadays would be 'No problem!'

Sr Teresa told me some years later what happened then. She sought out the Reverend Mother to tell her that I would soon be teaching her if she didn't do something about it. Even though nuns didn't travel alone in those days the Reverend Mother made arrangements for Sr Teresa to go by bus once a week for private lessons at the MacNamara School of Commerce in Waterford. There she was put right through the textbook and other books, and given plenty of homework but by now her star pupil was rapidly getting beyond the need for any tuition and was speedily moving himself into the accountancy area and loving it (her words!).

I made several attempts to pay for my tuition without success. But some years later (in the 1960s) I arrived with a payment which covered the amount I considered due, and this time I would not take no for an answer. Having at last broken the ice I brought various presents year after year as a gesture of thanks for what was done for me.

The other big religious occasion was Confirmation, which took place in Kill church in County Waterford in May 1947. It was my first time being in the presence of the Bishop of Waterford. Everyone who was confirmed also took the 'pledge' (to abstain from alcohol) up to the age of twenty-one. The pledge is still taken by children making their Confirmation in Ireland. To this day I have not broken my pledge not to drink alcohol.

The school had hurling and football teams in which I got involved. For this reason third, fourth and fifth class were great. Because arithmetic was my favourite subject I even went to the convent school in the evenings to study two subjects *not* on the Currabaha programme – algebra and geometry. Then sixth class arrived. But a problem developed. Our teacher, Sean Ormonde, became involved in politics and was elected to the Dáil (Irish parliament). We in sixth class had the problem. It was now January 1947 and our big primary examination was in June.

We had no idea what would happen to us without our teacher. In about mid-January a temporary teacher turned up. He lasted a couple of weeks. Then another came, a name I can remember, Mr Benson from Sligo. He lasted about ten weeks and introduced the school to Gaelic football. All the boys got on well with him. Between the time he left and examination time, we had two or three other teachers. One was a lady.

Anyway, getting towards examination time we had no idea how we would get on. The day finally arrived and the exams were held in the convent school. I had tried to keep up to date and can remember that when each paper was produced I was quite happy. When the results arrived I could not believe what I saw. Each paper had a maximum of 200 marks: total 600. My scores were: Arithmetic 190; English 169, Irish 147 – total 506. I was delighted. My homework must have done the job!

It was then suggested that I should take the scholarship examinations for St Augustine's Friary in Dungarvan. I did them and passed. Then the fun started. First of all, Dungarvan is thirteen miles from Kilmacthomas. It would mean two bus trips every schoolday, plus the cost of a uniform and books. On a postman's wages my parents reluctantly decided that they could not afford it. When the college was informed they would not accept it and on two (or was it three?) occasions, two representatives called to talk to my parents and myself. Each time they emphasised that because of my examination results and my love of sport, they wanted me. But with only my father's income to rely on my parents confirmed with regret that much as they would love me to go, financially it could not be done.

That was as near as I ever got to secondary school education in Ireland. When the summer holidays started some time in June 1949, I left school at the age of thirteen years and nine months. As a former schoolboy I enjoyed the rest of the summer with my friends – at the seaside, playing hurling and football. But at the beginning of September that came to an end. I then started to look for a job but without success. I suppose that at this stage of my life it did not even enter my head that getting a job would be so difficult. My initial enquiries were to businesses in Waterford and Dungarvan. No luck. Then my Uncle Paty suggested approaching Flahavan's factory in our own village, where he had been working since he left school. He knew I wanted an office job. I agreed to have a go. That was in mid-October 1949. I called into Flahavan's office and made an appointment for a few days later. My interview was with Tom Flahavan. He asked me to tell him what I was looking for. I said I wanted an office job and described what I was doing in the bookkeeping studies at the convent. His final reply was: 'I have no office work for you, but if you get in touch after the Christmas holidays I may have a vacancy in the mills.' I said to myself, 'Thanks, but no thanks.' I hadn't told my parents in advance about this meeting, hoping that I would be able to tell them that I had a job. Well, dreaming was free. When I told my father he said, 'If I had known about this job application, I would have told you to forget it.'

The months went slowly by. Christmas came, then the New Year. Nothing. It was very depressing. At last, some time in February I think, my father told me about a job coming up in the post office, a job as a telegraph messenger. The contract ended when the messenger reached the age of sixteen. I applied and with my dad's help got the post. Well, at least it was a job! I worked from Monday to Saturday from 10 a.m. to 7 p.m. A lot of hours, but it was not as bad as it sounds. Each day it was necessary to notify the post office that I was officially on duty, bring the post pffice bicycle and be ready to deliver telegrams. I had to be available all day, apart from lunch hour. When telegrams were received, a tap on the window would be my call. I would pick up the telegram, check the address and deliver it. The minimum post office charge was 3d (three old pence) for up to one mile.

I remember that the average charge was 9d (nine pence). Those journeys were my favourites because I was normally given a shilling, which meant that I could keep a 3d tip. At that time the telegrams brought news of births, marriages or deaths.

I had never been to a wake until one afternoon when I delivered a telegram. The person who answered the door said that the woman of the house had died and that the wake was on. I had to go in, kneel beside the bed where she was laid out and say a few prayers. I did. Not as frightening as I had imagined. The woman looked as if she was asleep. Going to farms where there were dogs was more frightening. The nearest I got to a problem was when an Alsatian caught a piece of the back of a raincoat that I was wearing. I got away before any real damage was done. The calls I liked least of all were ones to a country farm that came just before 7 p.m. on a dark winter's evening. My imagination used to run riot on the way home as I cycled as fast as I could. Delivering telegrams to houses where there was a new baby or where wedding celebrations were in progress was a much more enjoyable task. I was usually invited in for refreshments and asked to join in the festivities.

Once in 1951 there was a wedding reception at one house in Newtown where I delivered a telegram. The man of the house answered the door and when he saw me he said, 'Come on in. You will enjoy the reception for a while.' There was a nice crowd there enjoying themselves and probably by the end of the evening some of them would have been a bit under the weather. When people saw my Pioneer pin they offered me a cup of tea. Very nice. But then the father of the bride stood up said, 'We all know that Benny Beatty of Kilmac is a lovely singer. We are happy to have his son, Tony, in the house. He must be a chip off the old block. Give us a song, Tony.' I replied, 'You have the wrong fellow. I can't sing.' The response was 'You can't go until you sing.' I tried a cowboy song, finished it with my rubbish voice and left as quickly as possible, after my only ever solo.

Sitting and waiting to be called in to pick up a telegram in a small village and deliver it (something I experienced over a period of eighteen months) was a very boring existence. It was not always like that at the Kilmacthomas Post Office, as the following article from the *Munster Express* of 6 September 2002 shows:

On Christmas day 1929 – the day of peace and goodwill among men – Lawrence Griffin disappeared from the midst of his family in Kilmacthomas as effectively as if the ground of his native soil had opened and swallowed him. The only traces left behind him were the bicycle and postman's cape he had used that day bringing greetings and tokens of goodwill to his neighbours.

Lawrence was a popular man in the district and he was known far and wide because of his occupation, and when news of his disappearance became known the whole countryside turned out to help the Garda in their search for him. But it was all in vain in spite of the most intensive search over a huge area by squads of Garda drafted in from other adjoining areas and from Dublin itself.

The trail of Lawrence's deliveries that fateful Christmas day was checked and rechecked by the Garda and the last one was made in Stradbally. That was where he was last seen alive when his delivery was completed but from there on his movements were shrouded in secrecy. As time marched inevitably on rumours abounded, dark deeds were hinted at and strange theories abounded.

Hard facts were conspicuous by their absence apart from the news that a local farmer had found

Lawrence's bicycle and cape on a road about two miles from the village. In case he had fallen from his bicycle, been concussed and possibly confused and wandered into the nearby Glen Bog, a search was organised but to no good result.

Extra Garda officers and men were brought in from Waterford at first and later from all over the country to search far and wide. When newspaper reporters arrived in large numbers not just from all over Ireland but from abroad as well, the tension mounted and even General O'Duffy, the Chief Commissioner of the Garda, arrived in Stradbally to take command. The search was extended over a wider area and many graveyards were searched and graves dug up – greatly to the annoyance of people who had lost relatives in the recent past.

Then the search was widened to include the old copper mines at Tankardstown and the Bonmahon area generally. Despite their best efforts the Tankardstown mine only yielded up the carcasses of a few calves and pigs. The search was shifted to the Ballinasisla mine and special mining equipment procured from Waterford Harbour Commissioners but to no avail. Another switch was made to the slate quarries near Carroll's Cross on the main Waterford to Cork road and still no clues were found. As a last record every graveyard from the city to Dungarvan was searched with no result.

On 25 January two local men, a schoolteacher and a farmer, were arrested and charged with the murder of Lawrence Griffin. Three days later two other farmers from the locality were arrested and sensationally a mother, together with her young son and daughter, were arrested. All were charged with (a) unlawfully and feloniously murdering Lawrence Griffin (b) conspiring together secretly to dispose of the dead body of Lawrence Griffin.

When the accused appeared in Waterford Court on 14 February they were refused bail despite the fact that no body had been found. Two weeks later the ritual was repeated again and bail refused, with still no sign of a body. Searches at Coumshingaun lake in the Comeraghs and along the Mahon river proved fruitless. Finally on 7 March, Justice McCabe discharged all the prisoners and they naturally received a huge welcome back in Stradbally. But the question remains as to how eight people were kept in custody for so long for murdering a man whose body had not been found and which never did come to the light of day.

The above article does not explain how, for many years, it remained national news and, even now, in the early part of the new century is still an unresolved mystery. As the article above shows, Larry Griffin was a postman based in the Kilmacthomas post office. So was my father, who was a lodger at the time in my grandmother's house at 1 Millbrook Terrace. The Griffin family lived at No. 4. From now on, the account is made up of recollections of what my father said in my presence over the first ten or twelve years of my life. That is the reason I am able to discuss something which happened almost six years before I was born.

No doubt, as was normal, all the postmen got in early that Christmas day, sorted out their mail for delivery, wished each other all the compliments of the season, went on their routes and started their deliveries. They all returned safely, except

Larry Griffin, who had the Stradbally route. No messages were received from him. It was presumed that he had spent the night at a country house of one of his 'customers'. But there was no news the next day either. His family were getting concerned. The Garda were now involved and the search continued. Still no sign of him. That Christmas was, obviously, a desperate time for his wife and family. I realised that something serious had happened locally when, sometime before I was ten years old I heard my father talking to some locals. That was my first time hearing and understanding the words, 'missing postman'. Then, at the first available opportunity I asked my dad what it was all about. He told me quite clearly, in simple terms, what had happened. I found it very frightening, particularly when he explained that he had taken part in many search parties and that he was of the opinion that somewhere unknown a very serious accident must have occurred. And when it was realised that Larry Griffin was a veteran of the Boer War and the 1914–18 war it can be understood that he could have looked after himself. On many occasions I called to the Griffin house. They used to get two of the national newspapers every day and I used to enjoy them after school – particularly the sports pages. I can remember hearing that Mrs Griffin used to sit outside her front door in the summer evenings for some time after Larry's disappearance, in the hope that he might turn up one day. Alas it was a futile wait. The sad conclusion to this matter was that because her husband's body was never found his wife (widow) never got a widow's pension.

Around Christmas 1950, I got a wage increase to about £1/13s/9d (£1.69) per week. I continued giving my mother £1/10s (£1.50) s week and the extra few shillings helped me considerably, particularly as Kilmacthomas now had a very successful amateur dramatic group. The dramatic society had been going successfully for a few years before I got involved. It had a very good reputation throughout County Waterford and the south-eastern area. In

1951 members decided that some of their older players were about to move on so they approached some of the younger people in the area. I was one of those approached in August 1951. The idea interested me. I found the auditions fascinating. Anyway, after a couple of trials they told me that they had a production coming up called *Goodnight, Mr O'Donnell*, a three-act comedy by Robert Brennan. This would be the fourth production by the society and was due to be performed in November 1951. Whether or not it was in the interest of culture, or just for the fun of it, the society certainly got a great deal of credit for their efforts to keep the spirit of drama alive in mid-Waterford. The show was eagerly awaited and it received the same measure of support as was given to the three former productions.

My role in the play was that of a police officer, Sergeant Deegan. It appears that I carried out my role adequately and I had one experience that gave the audience an unplanned laugh. When we performed in Portlaw, a small town near Kilmacthomas, one of my moves was to come in the door and arrest a wrongdoer who was present. The door was too low and as I came in my cap hit the lintel and fell off. Although I was embarrassed, that episode brought an laugh from the audience. That was my only appearance with Kilmacthomas Amateur Dramatic Society and, apart from my appearance in 1956 at the St Alban's Garden Club, which I describe later on, I decided that amateur drama was not for me.

My post office work continued up to when I reached 16. Then the search for another job started. I had decided that I wanted on office job but I had no luck. I answered many advertisements and travelled to interviews but I got virtually the same reply all the time: 'Sorry, nothing available.' It was also quite clear that my lack of experience did not help – I was still only sixteen-and-a-half years old. Then a job came up in the village as assistant in a bar and grocery shop – Hills. I received an offer and took it just because I needed to do something. But the conditions were not good: I was to serve my time for three years as a barman (an excuse to pay low wages), working long hours and wages to start at 15s (75p) a week with regular reviews. Well, it was a job of sorts. I hoped that something better would turn up.

I continued in the job for over a year until I was sacked. I was leaving the shop on a Thursday evening, looking forward to a league soccer match that had been arranged. As I was going to the door the shop manager approached me and said, 'The confectionery van from Dublin is late. Can you wait for it? I replied 'I have a match at 7.30. I can only stay until 6.45.' He said, 'It should be here before that.' Then he went, leaving me to wait. At 6.45 the van had not arrived. I left then and played in the match. I cannot recall the score. However, the next morning Friday, was monthly fair day. It was usual to open the shop at 8.30 a.m. on fair days. I was there on time – but there was a welcoming committee waiting for me: the shop manager and the general manager. I was told that because I had not waited for the van on Thursday night, I was sacked. Big deal! My wages had increased to £1.75 per week.

I was idle for a few weeks. Then my dad told me that there was a vacancy in the post office for a temporary postman and I got the job. It was most enjoyable and when I got my first pay packet I knew that for the first time ever I would really be able to help my parents. For me the weekly wages were a fortune – £4/17s/ 6d (£4.87) a week. Over the next few months there was a lot of work to be done. One postman in particular was quite ill and as a result I got plenty of work. I still had time to get involved with my hobbies – football, reading, quizzes and dances. Yes, life was good, but still no sign of an office job. I kept trying – Waterford, Dublin, Cork, Limerick. No good. I realised that after another year if there was nothing I would have to cross over the sea to England.

In the meantime I worked away, played lots of football, went to many dances and did lots of competitions from the papers and the radio. My dad also enjoyed doing crosswords and competitions. One such competition which he got from Radio Luxembourg related to one of his favourite pastimes – horse racing. When I saw his entry form I decided to send for one. It arrived, I filled it up and posted it, some time in July 1954, and then forgot about it. In August, I was standing in for the postman on the Bonmahon route who was off sick. I was wandering down the beach, probably kicking a football, when I heard the call, 'Tony.' I looked up and saw my dad with two strange men at the entrance to the strand. I had no idea who they were and as I walked up to meet them I was totally puzzled. My dad said, 'These men want to talk to you about that racing competition with Radio Luxembourg. Do you remember it?' Of course I remembered. One of the men said, 'Can we get a private room in the pub? We want to ask you some questions.'

We went to the local pub, Kirwan's, and got a room. The questions started:

'What is your full name?'

'Bernard Anthony', known as "Tony" Beatty.'

'Did you do this competition?

'Yes.'

'Have you got a copy of your entry?'

'Yes.' I took it out of my wallet and handed it over. The two men examined it. One man said to the other, 'This looks like it.' Then he said to me, 'Having gone through all the entries in Dublin, we picked out this one as the winner. We called to your address in Kilmacthomas and asked your dad the same questions that we asked you. When we saw his entry form and checked it we realised that there was something wrong. We apologised to your father and when we were on our way to our car to begin the journey to Dublin your dad called us back and said, 'My son Tony also did this competition. His first name is also Bernard.' They then confirmed that my entry was the winner and told me that I would get a letter and cheque 'soon' from Dublin. They did not tell me how much I had won. I knew that £1000 was first prize, but I didn't dare dream.

Rumours went around the village about the amount I had won. I heard three figures at different times, £100.00 (the most popular figure), £250 and £500. Time went by. I heard nothing for many weeks. Then one morning in November I went into the post office at 6.30 as usual. All the postmen were there and, like me, sorted out the post for the different routes. I was on my way out when the postmaster, Tom Brown, called me and said 'There is a registered letter here for you. Go outside and open it.' I wondered why all the postmen, including my father, were still there. I soon found out. The letter contained a cheque, payable to me, for £1000! I had never seen so much money in my life. Payable to me! I called to my house, told my mother the good news and then went out to complete my route (I was on the Kill route). The postmaster had phoned the sub-post office with the news and when I got to the village of Kill there was a number of people waiting to congratulate me. Anyway, when I got back home I talked it over with my parents. We decided that the best thing to do would be for me to talk to a couple of local businessmen and to the bank and see what they would advise. I had meetings with Tom King, National Bank (now Bank of Ireland) and Sam Moore, Munster and Leinster Bank (now Allied Irish Banks). Apart from suggesting putting the money into their banks they had no other advice. I also spoke to a couple of local businessmen. No joy.

The advice I got suggested that I should put my winnings into the bank or the post office. I would get 2.5% or 3% interest there. Anyway I put it into the National Bank and told the manager that I would need to take some of the money out shortly. Two other matters then came up. My parents used to buy clothes for the family from Hadden's store in Dungarvan by opening an account and making weekly payments. I knew the effort made to organise those weekly payments. But they were paid and I found out that all payments were up to date. I told my parents to find out what was due and said that it would give me great pleasure to close it. I will never forget my mother's response to that. She said, 'Tony, that is too much.' I insisted and found out what was owed. It was something between £65 and £70. It gave me so much pleasure to clear this and to see how much it meant, particularly to my mother who dealt with it. It was when I was able to find out so little about what to do that I started to think that there was more to money than putting it into the bank or post office. I started to make enquiries and read books about what to do with money. I can categorically say that that was the reason that I started to learn about accountancy. But, at that time, in late 1954, I knew nothing about accountants or accountancy apart from Sr Teresa's comments at the convent school.

My temporary job as a postman had finished, so I again started looking for work. I still wanted an office job in Ireland and went to many interviews. But by Easter 1955, nothing had turned up. I played plenty of football with the local Kilmacthomas team. It was becoming clearer that unfortunately, for me, I would have to cross the Irish Sea to get a job. Kathleen and Paddy Kennedy, my aunt and uncle, were coming home as usual on holiday in June 1955. I had been in touch and agreed to think about going back with them to England.

All the planning then started. I was really going to miss my parents and family. But common sense clearly indicated that my country could not provide me with a job. There was just no choice. I did make a final effort to get something that would keep me at home but to no avail. Now I didn't need to think about it for long. There was no choice. Reflecting on my travels in Ireland I realised that I was quite inexperienced. I had been taken to Dungarvan and Waterford on occasions and my uncle Tommy who was a lorry driver once took me on a trip to Cork. Nothing more apart from job interview travels. Now I was to go on an entirely new trip. Living in a different environment is something I never had to consider. Then, finally, came the July date when I had to leave home for the first time. To appreciate what this meant, you would have to have been in a similar position.

In those days the *Great Western*, a passenger boat, went from Waterford to Fishguard. Most of the goodbyes were said at home but my father came with my aunt, uncle and myself in the hackney car to Waterford. Then the farewells concluded. I got on the boat with my aunt and uncle. The first couple of hours out of Waterford were, for me, exciting. Then to the cabin to retire for the night. I did not sleep much but thought about what I had done. For many, many years Irish emigrants had reluctantly left home to create a new life for themselves; I was now one of them and it was frightening.

Sleep came at last and when I awoke I was in a new country.

4

ENGLAND — AND HOME

When the boat arrived in Fishguard I was, I understand, asleep. My uncle had to call me. I woke up, got up, had a snack with my aunt and him, and then started the six-hour train journey to Paddington in London. Not seeing my mam, dad and family would take some getting used to. I was lucky to be with my aunt and uncle — they had been through this themselves a few years earlier. Without them I just do not know how I would have coped. Even small things counted like, for example, a cup of tea in a café at Paddington station. My arrangement was to stay with them until I got myself sorted out.

On Monday morning I had to face up to reality that now I was on my own. I got some local papers and started to study the employment situation. There were many office jobs advertised. But, as in Ireland, 'experience' was the key word. Finally I found a job advertisement which did not include the word 'experience'. I realised that I would have to start at the bottom in order to get the experience I so badly needed. The job I had in mind was with a company called the British Cardboard Box Machine Company Ltd. in St Albans. I phoned them up to make an appointment. No problem.

My appointment was with the company secretary, Mr Conquest. I was, I suppose, a bit apprehensive about the meeting although I realised that any jobs with figures involved would not create any problem. The job here was for a wages costing clerk. It was not the job I had in mind – I was hoping for an opportunity to work in the accounts office of a company. Anyway I was offered the job I had applied for at the massive salary of five guineas per week (£5.25). I objected but was told that with no office experience I could not get more. I told Mr Conquest that I would think about it and let him know in a few days. He said he would keep the job open for seven days but if somebody else suitable turned up he would take that person on. I was now in a 'Catch-22' position because I needed the experience.

For the next couple of days I tried a number of companies that had vacancies. In every case they were interested until the word 'experience' came up. Then it was a matter of, as in Ireland, 'Thanks but no thanks.' I had a couple of days plus the weekend to make a decision. Evetually I decided that after many months of failing to get a job in Ireland I would take what was on the table. At least it was a start. I then confirmed to Mr Conquest that I would take up the offer. So in late July 1955 my first job in England started. When I went in, all the details of the job were explained to me. I could not see any problem. I was also introduced to all the office staff and, as I was to deal with the wages, two foremen. They seemed to be a friendly lot. Anyway, the work went on and, as expected, I found it easy. In my own small way, I had become financially independent. But if my salary was anything to go by, the streets were not (as the song says) paved with gold.

After a few months I felt confident enough to leave the Kennedys' home. They had been extremely kind, refusing to take any money for my keep, but I was now twenty and felt it was time to discover what life had to offer a young bachelor without the constraints of family, no matter how well-meaning their advice. I took digs nearby, close enough to be in touch with them, but far enough away to be independent. I had also decided that, if I was going to get anywhere at all in accountancy, some sort of qualification was essential. I remembered the advertisements for correspondence courses which I had seen the previous year and decided to enrol at some stage. In the meantime, I got friendly with a few Irish lads whom I had met either at a social club or the church. Sometimes we discussed wages and the hurling and football matches in Ireland every weekend. Of the five that met fairly regularly, two were from Sligo, one from Galway, one from Cork and me from Waterford. We were all teetotallers and our main meeting place was a café. We played cards with low stakes. It was an Irish card game which was played under different names in different parts of Ireland. The game played in England was called Twenty-five, a form of whist. We usually had a session once a week from about mid-September to mid-April. When we started most of us were novices but by the time I returned home I was quite handy.

My four friends all worked in the building trade. A Gaelic football club, St Columcille's, was formed in St Albans. We all joined. I played a couple of games for them but I did not have the incentive to get totally involved. Wages became more of a priority, especially when I found out that all of my friends earned more than twice what I did. I was sorely tempted to join the building trade as a labourer. But after considering this I decided to stay in the job I was in. I had got an increase of five shillings a week in my wages, bringing my money up to £5/10/0 (£5.50). I asked Mr Conquest for a meeting about earnings. We met and I told him that if I couldn't earn more in that job I would have to leave and possibly join the building trade to get a decent wage. He knew that I was doing a good job and asked what figure I was looking for. I hopefully said eight pounds. He responded, 'I will talk to the directors. I think your figure is too high, but I will come back in a few days with a decision.' He called me into his office a couple of days later, as promised and told me, 'You are doing a good job but we cannot give you the figure you seek. Instead, we offer you a big increase to £7/10/0 (£7.50), payable immediately. Will you accept this?' I was elated. I accepted. That was the figure I was on until I returned to Ireland in May 1957. To me that additional two pounds made a big difference and for the first time I felt like a millionaire.

My football experiences during the above period, which covered two full seasons, are detailed below. First of all, my Uncle Paddy brought me to a league match at Kenilworth Road, Luton, between the home side, Luton Town, and Preston North End, in late August 1955. I remember thinking how different it was to the matches that I had watched in Kilcohan Park, Waterford. Knowing that I was interested in joining a club, Paddy also introduced me to a type of scout looking for new players for a Herts county league team, Colney Heath FC. He explained that they had two teams, one in the top division and the other in the second. He also told me that a club trial would be played on the Saturday and that I would be in the second team squad. It was a large squad but I was chosen for the first league match on the following Saturday.

A few interesting things happened in my first season. At most matches in the. county league, there would be scouts present from the senior amateur and professional clubs. The local senior club, St Albans City, were apparently impressed with my goal-scoring ability and asked my club if I could go for a trial. When I heard that I was, of course, delighted. I went for a trial match and it appeared that they liked me. I was chosen to play with their reserve side against Bromley in the Isthmian League on Saturday, 3 September 1955. We lost 1–0 but I, at number 11, had a good game. On the following Saturday, I was again chosen at number 11 in the league match against Ilford. This time we won 4–1 and I did what I was best at – scoring goals. I scored a hat-trick. At least

I had proved to myself and the club officials what I could do at a higher level of football.

At training on the following Tuesday, when the teams were selected for the following Saturday's matches, I went up to the notice board to confirm that I would be playing and to check the venue for the match. On the reserve side I was not mentioned. Then I thought that after my good display the previous Saturday, I must be in the first team which was not yet up on the notice board. I waited for the secretary to put it up. He did, and I checked it. I was not even mentioned. I found the secretary and asked him what was going on. He told me that a regular, on army service, was home for the weekend and needed a game. As I was the newest player it would be me who had to step down. But I told him that I was only interested in playing regular games of football. He accepted my comment and told me that I would definitely be in the following away match against, I think, Walthamstow Avenue. As a very active twenty-year-old, I could not take that and told him that unless my regular position could be guaranteed I would return to Colney Heath. His response was that no player could get such a guarantee. I stormed out and phoned the Colney Heath secretary. He said they would be delighted to have me back. I signed up with them again and for the rest of the season I alternated between the first team and the second team.

I had a wonderful first season away from home. I played in thirty-three matches and scored, believe it or not, forty-three goals. Both Colney Heath club teams won league medals but, as I played more games for the second eleven, I proudly ended the season with a Herts County League Division 2 medal, though in the cup competitions we were beaten in the early rounds. When I went home on summer holidays, my former club, Kilmacthomas, had a friendly match and asked if I would play. I said of course I'd love to play and really enjoyed being with 'the lads' again. It was good to be home.

Before I went on holiday a scout for a senior club, Hatfield Town, had asked me to consider joining them. I gave it a lot of thought and when I was at home on holiday I decided that I would accept their offer on my return. Another session with a senior team was a big bonus, particularly as I planned to return to Ireland at the end of the season. It was an interesting season. It started off with trial matches: first a general trial, then two first and second elevens matches. I played one match in each team. After that the real thing started. My first match was for the Second XI at home against Shefford town. We won by four goals to one of which I scored two. The next week we were away to Willesden Reserves. After being two goals to nil down, we recovered to draw 2–2. Again I scored both our goals. The next week I was promoted to the first team. It was away to Boreham Wood. We drew 2–2, but this time I did not score.

The following week I was retained in the first team and created a small piece of football history that will *never* to be equalled. Our opponents were Twickenham. The competition was the Parthenon League, (Premier Division). The headline on the local paper the following week read, 'Kick-off to first goal – ten seconds.' In fact the club historian who was in the stand told me after the match that it was scored in seven seconds. I scored that goal. The opponents kicked off first. I ran on the whistle, dispossessed them and slammed the ball to our left-winger. He ran a few steps, crossed it and I volleyed it from about 30 yards. It hit the net like a rocket. It was, I understand, the fastest goal ever scored in that league. The reason that this record will never be broken is because the league went out of existence some years ago and all the clubs joined other senior leagues.

Part way through the season a friend of mine who played in the first division of the Herts County League persuaded me to leave Hatfield Town and join his team, which was called Ballito Sports. My first game for them was with their second team, away to Royston Town Reserves. The standard was not great. Play went on and towards half-time there was no score. Then Royston got a penalty. The Ballito goalkeeper brought off a good save. He kicked the ball out towards midfield. I collected it and ran towards goal, hit a good shot and scored. So we were one goal up instead of one down at half-time. Great stuff! But in the first twenty minutes of the second half I scored five, yes five, goals. This obviously completely demoralised our opponents and just near the end, our right-winger scored to make the final score seven nil to us. I still have the programme and the newspaper cutting of that match. My team, Ballito Sports, finished runners-up in the first division of the Herts county league. So I ended up with a runners-up medal in the second division 1955–6 and the first division in 1956–7. Not a bad result from two memorable seasons.

In 1956 I had also joined a social club, the Garden Club in St Albans. They had a number of activities on offer, including language classes, a drama group and a table tennis club. Apart from a basic knowledge of Irish I had no further interest in languages although I did sit in on a few French and German classes.

The club had a number of table tennis teams, all entered in the St Albans and District Table Tennis League. I decided to have a go at it. For a few months before the season started I spent a lot of time practising and found that I got up to the standard of the lowest division team, the Garden Club's 'C' team that played in the fourth division of the league. It was a pleasant addition to my football. When the league started I was ready and I was picked for the first match. There were twenty-two teams in our division. That meant twenty-one matches home and away – a total of forty-two matches. Each match consisted of two singles and one doubles so the total number of matches that could be played by an individual player was sixty-three – forty-two singles and twenty-one doubles. Believe it or not I was the only player to take part in as many as sixty-three matches. My record was as follows: singles: won twenty-one and lost twenty-one; doubles: won nine and lost twelve.

I was quite happy with that record but the season did not end there. At my workplace annual competitions were held in darts, dominoes, snooker and table tennis. I entered the MacFie Cup table tennis competition. There was a good entry and each round was for the winners of the best of three games. Believe it or not I won the MacFie Cup the first time I entered it. My apprenticeship with the Garden Club's table tennis club had paid dividends.

The trophy was presented at the company's annual dinner but before my return to Ireland I gave back the perpetual Cup and kept the replica, which made a lovely souvenir. As I had seen some of the superstar table tennis players in action it was quite clear to me that to reach something like their standard it would have been necessary to have started playing at a very young age and to get proper coaching. So that game was not for me but, again, one could dream!

Looking back I can see that table tennis and football were nice pastimes for a young, single man. Knowing that I would be returning to Ireland (as I thought forever) come May 1957, I just wanted to pass the time as comfortably as I could, until that date.

I got involved in one other venture, this time with the Garden Club's Little Theatre Group. All the planning had been done for their 1956 production – a play called *Count Your Blessings*. I got involved with the group for a strange reason. When I saw their rehearsals going on at the club, I must have mentioned to somebody that I had taken part in a play in Ireland before I emigrated. Everything seemed to be going well until one of the senior members had to cry off because of appendicitis. There was panic. Numerous enquiries of club members were made with no success. Eventually I was approached – in desperation, I think! I refused at first but many refusals later I thought that as I used the club so much I would be pestered until I said yes. Because of the other activities I was involved in – football and table tennis – there would have to be conditions. I told the theatre committee that I had very little experience but to help them out I would give it a go if the rehearsals did not affect my football or my table tennis. On Tuesday and Thursday nights I would attend the club for rehearsals but on match nights I would be missing. Because of their dilemma they agreed.

I worked hard at my lines – the budding accountant had no problem there. But then the real problems started. In the weeks leading up to opening night all the players, except me, worked on rehearsals each night. Almost every night when I came late I had to remind them of their promise to me and to tell them that although I knew how important the play was to them, it was only number three among my recreational activities.

They found that hard to take despite my confident predictions that it would be 'all right on the night'. The rehearsals continued. I found them to be fairly easy and as the opening night got closer I realised that although some of the actors and actresses seemed to be fairly apprehensive, I had no fears. The first performance was a press night and the local newspapers had their reporters and photographers present. Although I was used to having the press at football matches this was new to me. The easiest way to highlight the way that the play was reported is to reproduce part of the report from one of the local papers, the *Herts Advertiser*:

So many things went amiss prior to the opening of Ronald Jean's *Count Your Blessings* at the Garden Club, St Albans, that the title might have very well expressed the feelings of everyone concerned in the production. The club's Little Theatre Group could certainly count their blessings that a beginning was made at all. Misfortune in large doses has dogged the company ever since August last year when a tree crashed through the roof, wrecking the stage and damaging scenery and lighting equipment.

It took longer than expected to replace the equipment and repair the stage and have it ready for use again. Planned for early December, *Count Your Blessings*, the first production of the season, had to be put off for eight weeks.

The producers, Patrick and Moyra Willis, had further problems to combat with a necessary last-minute change in the cast. Tony Beatty took over the part of Theodore Malek with very little rehearsal time left, and was to be commended on his performance when the play opened on Wednesday.

The newspaper story was much longer than this. One photograph of the production appeared in the paper: me in my costume and beard with one of the actresses in a scene from the play! Looking back I consider my spell in amateur dramatics just to have been an interesting passing phase. And more than anything I had done ever done before, this was very much a case of 'quitting when you are ahead'. I was ahead and I did quit.

On 16 May 1957 I returned home – for good, as I thought. Well, as I have often said, dreaming is free! I spent a couple of weeks' holiday renewing life with my parents, sisters, brother and other relatives and friends. Settling in at home again was a most enjoyable time. I then started to look for a job. Of course as one with office experience I had high hopes. After a few negative enquiries – success. I got an interview for a job as assistant to the accountant in Carrick-on-Suir, a town about twelve miles from my home. The business had a number of retail shops in various towns and villages within about a twenty-mile radius. At the interview I understood that at first my job would be to assist the accountant to provide weekly accounts for each shop and quarterly accounts for the group. The basis was there for a long-term position. I was offered a wage of £6/10s (£6.50) per week, which I accepted. I started but then found out that the reality was a bit different from what I had been told. I learned that the accounts for the whole operation were about two years in arrears and that no arrangements had been made for interim accounts. My instructions then changed. I was told to help bring the arrears up to date and prepare weekly accounts for each shop.

I enjoyed the work and took lodgings locally. The local scene became well known to me. I even took part in an indoor five-a-side soccer tournament held in the local dance hall. I was really settling down and then on 31 July 1957, the most important thing in my life happened. The occasion was the weekly dance in the local dance hall. I met my wife, Breda, there and from the beginning I knew that I had met somebody special. A native of Listowel, County Kerry, Breda, who was a schoolteacher, had moved to Carrick-on-Suir to be with her mother and sister after the death of her father in Kerry a few months earlier. He was a native of Carrick-on-Suir.

The next few months were idyllic, while we got to know each other better. At that time I thought about buying a second-hand car. I went with my father to have a look at some in a few garages in the area. I finally found one that I liked. It was a Morris Minor, (KI 5206) at Hornibrook's Garage in Lismore. I told them that I would take it a few days later when I had organised car insurance and a driving licence. The insurance was organised and then I called into a post office and bought a driving licence. Yes, it was as easy as that – no test and no formalities – just call in with the money and go out with a full driving licence. I took a few driving lessons with my brother-in-law, Matt Lonergan, and when I felt confident enough to drive I was able to drive to work every day. For a couple of months I did that, met Breda most evenings, and then drove home. After some time, I felt that I was getting on very well at work, able to cope well with whatever was passed on to me so I decided to buy a new Ford Prefect. This car cost £750.00 and was paid for as follows; the Morris Minor, plus £200.00 cash was the deposit and the balance of £350.00 was on hire purchase. The car registration number was KI 7591. I had a few very good months with this car.

Christmas 1957 came and went. I had met Breda's mother and then during the Christmas holidays I introduced Breda to my parents. After the holidays, work on the accounts continued apace and by the third week of January 1958, we had brought the annual accounts up to date and the interim weekly accounts system was ready to operate. Then came February. I was very pleased with the way my work was going. My boss sent for me to attend a meeting. This was good news and I thought that the meeting was to congratulate me on a job well done and to offer me a pay rise and explain what I would have to do from now on. Not at all! I was told that as the big job was now up to date, my services would no longer be required. Despite my protests about the promises now being broken, I was told that there was no record of them made and I got a week's notice.

My return to Ireland ended in the way many people had told me that it would, with no job. But more importantly, not being in the town as my girlfriend Breda was something that I had not anticipated. We had just recently got engaged. Of course, having a car meant that we were still able to meet regularly. No jobs were available. I tried hard, even went as far as Dublin for interviews, but the answer was always the same. No. During the school holidays at Easter Breda and I went to Kerry for a lovely few days holidays. Kerry is such a beautiful county. Driving up the famous

Conor Pass was something that I will never forget.

It was becoming more and more obvious that I would have to return to England. Only my family and I knew how much I wanted to stay in my own country but it was not to be. I finally, very reluctantly, returned to England in June 1958. Breda came over when the school summer holidays started and stayed with her sister in Kentish Town. This time I decided to settle in north London. I stayed with friends until I found suitable lodgings. In the meantime, I saw some job vacancies in the local newspaper. I made an appointment with an accountancy firm in Kilburn. Their office was above a butcher shop on the High Road. The boss was also managing director of the company which owned the shop and a group of other butcher shops mainly in the north London area. Apart from work in the practice, this job included preparing a weekly profit-and-loss account for each of the shops. Anyway, I got the job. The weekly wages were the highest I had ever earned: £15 per week. When I got the required training from the boss, this job was really good. I loved the work.

In August, 1958, I was introduced to the secretary of Blackburn Football Club, who worked as a butcher in one of my boss's shops. When he found out that I played football and was looking to join a club he brought in a membership form and signed me on straight away. However, I still had to find lodgings and here I had problems. I made some phone calls but came up against the main obstacle of the time: 'No Irish or coloured need apply.'

I finally got a positive reply from a foreign lady – French, I think. I made an appointment to call to her address – just off Kilburn High Road – within a day. When I called, and before she showed me the room, she told me that she had Irish tenants in her large three-storey house. I was hopeful as I followed her up the stairs to the third floor. We came to a door and she told me to be quiet as we went inside. There was a large quilt handing across the room. After showing me the part of the room without a bed she told me that the bed was behind the quilt. I looked there, saw the bed and a man asleep in it. I asked what was happening. She said, 'I have a number of people like him. They work at night and sleep during the day. When you get home from work the man will be out and the bed will be clear. So you will have no problem.' I told her that I would want my own room, so my response to her was, as so often, 'Thanks, but no thanks.'

In desperation, I decided to go to the Catholic church in Quex Road, Kilburn. I told the priest about my dilemma. He answered, 'We're in luck, I think. A Tipperaryman, a parishioner here, called a few days ago and told me that he and his wife had decided to let one of their rooms, now that their grown-up family had moved out. He asked me to phone if I found a suitable person.' The priest phoned his parishioner and arranged a meeting. I saw the room, took it and had a most enjoyable few months there.

By the time Breda went back to recommence her teaching in Clonmel, we had decided on our wedding date, Easter Monday, 30 March 1959. During the following few months my work continued to go well and so did my football. Then in early December, I was approached after Mass by the secretary of St Mary's football club. He asked me if I would be interested in joining them until the end of the season and told me a few things about the team. They were associated with the social club at the church and at that time they were members of the first division of the Hendon and District football league. They were the unbeaten leaders. I had been recommended to them. When I heard that, at that time, it was legal to play in Saturday and Sunday competitions I was very pleased to sign up. There were seven league matches still to play.

5

MARRIED LIFE

Our wedding day, Easter Monday, 30 March 1959, finally arrived. I remember travelling with my parents from our home in Kilmacthomas to St Peter and Paul's Church in Clonmel. Breda was taken to the church from her mother's home in Carrick-on-Suir by her brother, Sean. The Mass and the wedding ceremony were carried out by local priest, Fr Meehan. Breda's sister Mairead was her bridesmaid and my best man was my schoolfriend and next-door neighbour, John Foley.

We enjoyed a lovely reception in Hearn's Hotel, Clonmel. After the ceremony and celebrations we caught a train to Dublin, then a cab to the airport. Neither of us had ever flown before so we were very excited about our journey to Paris via Heathrow. Paris in the springtime was magical. We enjoyed a cruise on the river Seine, toured all the famous sights in the greater Paris area, visited to the Eiffel Tower and the rest and savoured the French food. The week just flew by and it was time to return to London the following Saturday. There we took up residence in a rented double room in Cricklewood, north-west London.

On our return there was some post waiting for me. This included a postcard from Blackburn FC, my Sunday football club in Kilburn. It said that I had been chosen as centre-forward for the Kensington league cup final to be played the following day.

Not the return that I hoped for! Anyway, I turned up, played an excellent match and scored a second-half goal in a 2–0 victory over a tough Porchester Athletic side. Then it was back to work from Monday morning,

I visited some estate agents and got a number of catalogues. We also found out that the deposit for a house purchase was 10% of the sale price. Therefore the most sensible purchase price for us was £3000 maximum. There were many properties in the price range that we could afford. We started viewing in early July and finally got one that we both liked in mid-August. The address was 101 Turner Road, Queensbury, Edgware, Middlesex – a three bedroomed end-of-terrace house. The price was £2,900. For an extra £250 we got it fully furnished and that was the main reason that we chose it. The finance was arranged as follows: £300 deposit was the amount I had left from the £1000 which I had won in 1954. The £250 for the furniture came from our savings, which at that time amounted to just over £400. The balance was lent by Westbourne Park Building Society and the monthly repayments were £17.02. My salary at that time as a trainee accountant and as a clerk to the accountants' other business, was £15 per week. The first two building society annual statements show that the total payments were £408.40. Of that total just over £313 was interest and the insurance £4.80. When all that was dealt with it meant that after two years, the balance due was more than £2500. Not very encouraging! But on the plus side we had a few lovely years there. From 28 September 1959, when we first moved into the house, it was a lovely feeling – our own house!

The time was coming up for me to start my course at the Kilburn polytechnic. I went there straight from work, had time for a cup of tea and then the lectures started. With this on Mondays, Wednesdays and Fridays, plus the correspondence course, I would be ready for the intermediate accountancy examinations. I carefully considered the dates. I had intended to sit one in December 1959 but decided that as the intermediate examinations were to be on different dates in June 1960, I cancelled my December 1959 date and decided to do both examinations in June 1960. The dates of the finals in June 1961 and June 1962 would not change.

Then, on 8 February 1960, our baby, Catherine Mary, arrived. I can only describe this as a really wonderful event. Because it was something so totally new to us, Catherine's arrival changed our lives.

The 1959-60 football season was, for me, a non-event. I played a few games for St Mary's early in the season and because of the changes in my personal life, decided to take it easy. Over the 1959 Christmas holidays I was approached after Mass one Sunday by a stranger who told me that he was the secretary of Greenmount Celtic, a club who played in the Harlesden Sunday Football league, He was very flattering to me. He had heard of my goal scoring feats and knew I was not signed on for any Sunday club that season. He told me that his club was an inexperienced side and asked if I would play a few matches in the league and in the forthcoming Dwyer Cup competition. He was aware that the standard of the division that they played in was much lower than what I was used to but if I played he said that it would be a great boost for the club. As there was no further obligation at the time I decided to play but not at number nine. That was agreed. I took part in five league matches and five cup matches for them, but none in my favourite position. The club ended the season about midway up the table but the cup competition had some very good matches. I enjoyed it and for the record scored eight goals there.

The final versus Collars was about the worst game of football I had ever played or taken part in. I just could not get going and in the end I was pleased to see the finish of it. The 3–0 defeat was better than we deserved. The replica cup that we all got was a souvenir that brings back bad memories. So goodbye 1959–60.

Getting out with Breda and our little girl, Catherine, was lovely. Watching her development was really special. Day by day, seeing her progress at home and on outings was, of course, something new and wonderful to Breda and myself.

In June 1960, after my intermediate examinations, my parents came over from Ireland to us for a holiday. I shall never forget their excitement. My mother had been to England for a period before she went home and married my father, but it was my father's first trip outside Ireland. Knowing his love of horse racing, I arranged to take him to Epsom on Derby Day. He really enjoyed that day out and so did I. Finding winners, though, was not easy. I cannot remember if I backed a winner. I mustn't have done so because I returned home with less money than I started with. My father did not have any luck either. But, anyway, we had a great day out. As my father said afterwards, 'Just to be able to say I was at the races in Epsom on Derby Day is, for me, the big news.' I was so proud of being able to do that for him but I wasn't finished yet. I remembered those Saturday nights when my dad used to go out for his regular trip to Waterford Kilcohan Park for the greyhound racing, known as 'the dogs'. I used to look forward to Sundays when, after Mass, my dad used to give me the programme of the Saturday meeting, known as the 'dog card', and a bundle of coloured cards. I used to enjoy those cards until my dad told me that bringing home a lot of cards indicated that he had lost more than he wished.

Breda took my mother out on a few shopping trips and she loved it while I arranged for my dad to come to a few 'dog' nights. We went first of all to the White City. We booked a table in the restaurant there and it was lovely to pick out our choices and have someone come to take our bets while we watched the races from our table. We both enjoyed this and ended up that night with more winners than losers. We went to two other meetings before my parents went home. One was at Wembley and the other was at

Walthamstow. Over the three meetings we about broke even. This was an excellent experience and we both enjoyed each outing. My parents both enjoyed the holiday and returned home with them happy memories, laden with presents for the rest of the family at home.

My work and my accountancy studies were going quite well. I did the examinations in June and having no problems dealing with the questions, I expected to pass. The results I expected came in mid-August. So I was now ready to prepare for the finals. I started back at the Kilburn polytechnic when it re-opened in September 1960. I decided that I would carry on there until June 1961 when I would sit the International Accountants final and then in June 1962 I would tackle the exams for the Institute of Certified Public Accountants in Ireland. The polytechnic studies plus the School of Accountancy work would help me to get through both.

Meanwhile my football career continued. First of all in June and July 1960 I togged out for a few Gaelic football matches. A friend of mine played for a London senior club, the Shamrocks. He asked me if I would like to join them and play a few games for them. So I agreed and played three games for them – all at New Eltham. I then decided to concentrate on soccer. The 1960–61 soccer season was fast approaching. I had decided to join the local senior club, Edgware Town, for Saturday matches. The club had three teams, the first one playing in the Corinthian senior league. They also had two reserve sides; one played in the Corinthian reserve league and the other in the Harrow, Wembley and District league, division one. My aim was to get into one of those latter two sides in order to gain access to the club's coaching and training facilities. After a couple of trial matches, it was decided that I would take the centre-half-back position in the side taking part in the Harrow, Wembley and District league and I was also the reserve centre-forward. This suited me.

Now that the Saturday position was sorted out, it was time to organise the Sunday situation. An Irish football friend, Phil McCabe, from Dundalk, suggested that we should consider putting an all-Irish Sunday league team into the Kensington league. He said that he had already spoken about this to some of his colleagues. He and I then sat down and worked out the plans for such a project. We found out that, at that time, we knew of about fifteen Irish players who we felt could be coaxed into playing. We then had a preliminary meeting with as many players as we could find. They all thought that this was an excellent idea. My friend, Phil, then said, 'Tony, I had another meeting with the lads and we came up with the following notion: you were through all this in Ireland. If we take over all the secretarial work we suggest that, with your experience, you take over as manager, player and captain. What do you think?' My reply was: 'I like the idea. So long as you are all in favour, I will have a go – but for one season only.' We then applied to the Kensington league and got into the second division, where I had played two seasons before.

We registered a club name which embraced both Irish football traditions – Shamrock Rangers. We managed to get a poor second-hand set of jerseys from one of our club acquaintances. It was now about mid-August and the local Kensington newspaper got in touch with us. Three of us met the reporter. He told us that every season the paper picked out a team to give good coverage to. He said that they had heard so much about us they decided that, although we were a new side to the league, they would pick our side for big coverage in 1960–61. To us this was great. After my exam results arrived in August I started to prepare for the first final exam in June 1961. My study plans were as follows, fitted into a working week of 9 a.m. to 5.30 p.m. on Monday, Tuesday, Wednesday and Friday, 9 a.m. to 1 p.m. on Thursday and 9 a.m. to 12.30 p.m. on Saturday:

Monday 6.30–9.30: polytechnic
Tuesday 7.30–9.00: football training;
10.00–midnight: correspondence course
Wednesday 6.30–9.30: polytechnic
Thursday 7.30–9.00: football training
10.00 – midnight: correspondence course
Friday 6.30–9.30: polytechnic
Saturday am: relaxing with family
pm: playing football match in season
Out of season: relaxing
Sunday am: church and football
pm: playing a football match

I spent a lot of time with my family at the weekends and a short time on the correspondence course. Of course during the season it was football (soccer) on Saturday afternoons and Sunday mornings. When football was on Sunday mornings I got Mass on Sunday evenings. My work was developing well – certainly doing the weekly accounts for the shops was a useful exercise for me.

After the completion of the 1960–1 season it was all systems go for my first accountancy final in early June 1961. This examination would be held in a large office building in the City of London. But, in the meantime, the studies continued remorselessly. The subjects, some the same as for the intermediate examinations, were of a much higher standard but I was getting on well with them. At the polytechnic and on the correspondence course I did many tests, but had no difficulty handling them. The examination date finally arrived. I sat it and, when it was over, I felt confident that I had done well enough to pass. The results would come out two months later – in about the second week of August.

I had changed my job and was now assistant to the accountant for a firm of insurance brokers in Edgware. At that time I knew very little about insurance. During my sojourn there, about six months, I gained useful knowledge about employers' liability, public liability, vehicle insurance, property insurance and all types of cover – certainly something that everybody in business should have an idea of.

I gave some thought to my football position for 1961–2, but this was not straightforward. My main aim was to be ready for the final examinations of the Institute of Certified Public Accountants in Ireland. Although the International Accountants examination finals results would be a little while longer I decided to take the Irish Accountancy body's examinations as my priority and, at this stage, hope that the results of the International Accountants body would be good and that I would not have to start getting ready again for the examinations in December. I decided not to do anything about my recreation, football, until I got the accountancy result in a few weeks. I did, however, play a few Gaelic football games which, if nothing else, showed how unfit I was.

The Shamrock Rangers position needed to be clarified. The committee members came to meet me in the hope that I would be available in 1961–2 despite the fact that I had pointed out quite clearly at the start of the 1960–1 season that I would be available only for that season. We all agreed that the club's first season was very successful and the committee said that they needed me in the first division. I re-emphasised that, as promised, I would be available only for a handful of matches. The fact that I needed more time with my family and also had an important examination coming up meant that everything else was secondary. They realised, finally, that I would not be available. The letter from the Association of International Accountants finally arrived. Although I felt quite confident regarding the result, I must say that I opened the letter apprehensively. Yes, the good news was there. I had passed and was now a qualified accountant. I just could not wait to let my parents know.

In September 1961, I started the Kilburn polytechnic course, which, alongside my School of Accountancy course, would be the last of my studies when I sat the final for the Institute of Certified Public Accountants in Ireland the next June. My work on the courses was going quite well and I suppose that having passed all my examinations to date at the first attempt was a good boost for my confidence. Not having had a football match for some time gave me the feeling that something was missing. I bumped into an acquaintance who played for a senior club, Rayners Lane, of the Spartan League, and discussed football in general. He knew that I was missing the game and suggested that I go out with him to the club's ground on the next training night to see how I got on. He also mentioned that there were a couple of trial matches coming up, first team against second team. He suggested that if I would like to get on to one of the sides, he would put in a word for me.

At the next training session the club manager called me and said, 'I know your history and your present position from your friend. I have a new defender joining the club within the next three months. Would you sign on for a few months? Apart from that I will not call on you and, of course, you will have access to our training facilities until the end of the season.' With no permanent commitment, I agreed. This brought me up to almost the New Year 1962. In fact I played ten matches, all at centre-half back, for the club. The first five matches were for the reserve team and then I was promoted to the first team. The competitions I played in were the FA Amateur Cup, the Middlesex Intermediate Cup and Spartan League. My playing term then ended and for the remainder of the season it was training only.

Christmas 1961 was very special, being Catherine's second Christmas. She was nearly two now and, although she didn't really understand about Father Christmas yet, he came and brought her presents. Breda and I delighted in seeing her face when she opened her presents. And, of course, she loved the fairy lights and Christmas decorations. That was not all the good news: our next addition to the family was to be in July 1962; a sister or brother for Catherine.

The studying was going very well and a few people who heard that I was qualified approached me to take on their work. But I emphasised that I was not ready yet to do so. Also, I tried another job. This time it was for an accountancy agency that passed out jobs to qualified accountants on a self-employed basis. The great thing about this operation was the fact that I could choose when I wanted to work, which meant that, despite the fact that I was very up-to-date with the Kilburn polytechnic lectures, I could also spend as much time as I needed on the School of Accountancy course.

Having already qualified as an international accountant I felt very confident going into the finals of the Institute of Certified Public Accountants in Ireland. All the hard work over the previous few years would, I hoped, give me the qualification I hoped for. It certainly gave me the feeling that I would get through. At this stage I had got on to the Association of International Accountants to seek a practising certificate. But before it arrived, the examinations had to be done. No subject paper I took caused me any problem. In fact, going back through the papers, I confidently expected to pass. I was now able to review my position. No more examinations, I hoped. Breda was taken into Edgware General Hospital during the second week of July and Claire was born on the fourteenth – a sister for Catherine.

I carried on with agency work until the end of July while I made up a list of the clients who I knew wanted me to act for them. This was the real beginning of the Beatty & Company practice. In mid-August, I got the long-awaited letter from Dublin and the news was good! I could now, having formally complied with all the requirements, apply for membership of the Institute of Certified Public Accountants in Ireland. A dream come true!

From early 1962 onwards, the idea about having a go on my own started to develop. By mid-1962 my private work was getting quite extensive and the records I was taking in were getting to the point where the space I had available was becoming too small. Building a list of clients started to get hectic and now it was time to look for office accommodation. As quite a lot of the cases that I had were in north London this was the area in which I looked for an office. After looking at a few places I finally became a tenant at 547 Holloway Road, London N19. My first employee was a secretary. At the time I realised that with all the letters I had to deal with urgently, that was one position which would not be idle. My first tenancy was for twelve months. The landlord was a very nice person. When we met he was most helpful and said that he could remember what it was like when he started off. He said that if I had a problem when the rent was due I should talk to him. He also said that if the practice got busier he had another room available. Things got very busy and I took the second room and employed my first accounts clerk.

My very first client was a man who worked as a butcher in the company I worked for in Kilburn. He had kept in touch and when he left his job and took over the lease of a butcher's shop in Kentish Town it was obvious that he would ask me to act for him. That was in April 1962. Another interesting early case was when I was approached after Mass one Sunday by a stranger who said that he was looking for an accountant and heard that I had started in practice. He had two furnished houses for letting and asked if I would take on his business. I was happy to do so.

Two of the building contractors and one of the haulage companies that had promised their business to me when I got office accommodation came in with their documents in late

October and early November 1962. The word got around that I dealt with those businesses and others contacted me. So coming up to Christmas 1962 I had many cases and was delighted with the way things were developing. I had enough work to keep me going for about five or six weeks and with the promises I had of other work I could not see any problems ahead. But read on...

Over Christmas it started snowing. No problem, I thought. After all, most years we had snow for a day or two. But Christmas 1962 was different. After the holidays the snow just continued. At New Year every place was white. The television and the newspapers indicated that it would not last 'much longer'. But the end of January came, then the end of February and still plenty of snow. Then economic problems started – a lot of the people in the building trade could not work and, as a result, could not pay their accountant (me). This continued – what a time to start a business! Finally, in March, 1963, I had to to get a job, with any luck I hoped for only a few months. This was a time when being a qualified accountant helped. I got a temporary job in the accounts department of a large retail store not far from where we lived. Of course, football was out though I did continue training. Anyway by June, the weather was normal. I approached the head of the department where I worked to thank the company for the work and he offered me a permanent job there. He said that the company liked my work and would like me to consider the offer. I told him, though, that I proposed to work at developing my practice. The builders started to work again and I got so busy that I had to employ another accounts clerk in late June 1963.

As the new cases started to come in they included a lot of tax work. Despite the weather, the Inland Revenue wanted tax returns and payments on account when tax assessments had been raised and not appealed against. There was plenty of work and I had to increase my staff again. The public relations work that I took on was becoming busier and busier. I had never known anything like this before. I really enjoyed the work with the Inland Revenue. Getting in touch with bank managers and clients was quite interesting.

In June 1964 we sold our house in Queensbury, Edgware, for what was, at that time, a fortune, £5000. We then returned to Ireland – to Dublin – in August 1964. We moved into the Montrose Hotel, Ballsbridge, Dublin, began our search for a new house immediately and found one in Foxrock. Before I returned to London we arranged for Catherine to go to school in the Dominican convent, Dun Laoghaire. Breda was expecting our third child around Christmas.

Our plan was that I would keep the accountancy business going in London and commute fairly regularly to Dublin. I would also keep my eyes open for a possible accountancy vacancy in Dublin. I went back to London on 8 October 1964 to continue with my work. My secretary had made two appointments for me with potential new clients. I met them within my first week back. I will never forget those two cases who after our meetings became clients. Both had been recommended by existing clients. That list was getting bigger and the workload was challenging. I was enjoying it, and taking work to my digs at night was not unusual. At the end of October it was time to go to Dublin for a break. Breda and Catherine met me at the airport. Settling in with Breda, Catherine and Claire in Foxrock was tremendous. Taking them out on family outings was most enjoyable. For me, particularly, the time passed too quickly. I phoned my office in London evey day while I was away and was kept up to date by my secretary. I found that, even when I was in Dublin, the practice kept getting busier.

My next trip home was on 15 December. The first couple of days were just relaxation. I spent a day in Waterford with Catherine, to visit my parents and exchange Christmas presents. Then back to Dublin where I enjoyed a few days with the family.

Breda was taken to the Coombe Maternity Hospital in Dublin. Both Catherine and Claire were excitedly looking forward to their mum coming back home with a new brother or sister for them. In the meantime, Father Christmas visited on Christmas Eve and brought them the presents they had hoped for. So we all enjoyed Christmas and looked forward to the expected new arrival. On 26 December, Paul Anthony, our eldest son, arrived. Our family was now five – Catherine, Claire, Paul, Breda and I.

Into the New Year of 1965, and I was really enjoying the time with my family but I had to arrange to return to work in London. I had been informed by my secretary that the office was very busy and that she had made some appointments for me to be dealt with on my return. The first appointment was on 22 January with an existing client. I returned to London on the twentieth, very reluctantly, I must admit. Before I came back I made some enquiries about the possibilities of getting a job at home but the much-cherished hope, that more opportunities might have opened up in Ireland, fell flat. Nothing had changed. Just as well that I had kept the practice going in London. It was 'all go' there and the business was, in fact, improving and developing.

My prison experience happened in March 1965 during the period when my family lived in Ireland and I was over and back regularly. I usually stayed in a small hotel in north London when I was away from the family. After my day's work in my office – at that time my offices were at 246 Hornsey Road, London N7 – I went back to the hotel for an hour or so, before going out to a restaurant to have dinner with a prospective new client. As I left the hotel I told the owner, who that night was acting as doorman, that I did not know what time I would be back. He replied that there was no problem. I had an excellent meal and discussion with my companion, who had a company in the building trade. He became a client and his business was most successful. He remained with me until he returned to Ireland with his family in the early 1980s. That night in London we went back to my new client's house and continued with our chat. It was about 11.30 when the meeting broke up and I reached the hotel around midnight.

When I went up the steps to open the front door I found it locked. Many knocks later it was obvious that nobody was going to respond. What to do now? I drove up to Hornsey Road police station to seek help. I didn't know if they could help – it was merely a shot in the dark. The officer in charge, realising how frustrated I was, asked me to follow him downstairs. He showed me a couple of empty cells and said, 'This is where we hold overnight prisoners but as tonight is a quiet night you can spend the night in one of the cells until we begin a new shift at 7.30 in the morning. We will call you some time between 6.30 and 7.00.' My only night spent in a police cell was very peaceful. When I got up before 7.00 I was given a cup of tea and left the station before the new shift started. I went to my office at about 8 o'clock, went through the telephone directory, found a few north London rental agencies and got myself organised in another small hotel. During the day I called up to the address of the hotel of which I was locked out in order to settle my account. Believe it or not they attempted to charge me for the night I was locked out. They finally saw sense and accepted the week's payment less one night. So ended an extraordinary night's fun.

I missed the family and realised that much as my kids looked forward to my trips home, I looked forward to them even more. My next trip home was on 12 March. The festivities for St Patrick's Day were just starting. As a family (all five of us), we enjoyed the events. I began to think again about what it would be like to live at home. But no luck. I even tried to get involved in a practice just starting out. But after a while I realised that this would not work. Getting a job in the Dublin area was not on.

While I was away from London, my secretary put into

practice a system that enabled me to deal with outstanding correspondence. I used a Dublin agency to deal with my correspondence from Ireland. I set up one of my employees in London – a qualified accountant – to deal with all taxation work with the other staff. I agreed an increase in his salary with which he was quite happy. 5 April came and went. Since all the London work was being dealt with, I was able to spend a lot more time at home with the family. I suppose I was still clinging desperately to the hope that better times for Ireland were just around the corner. I was wrong. I returned to London on 12 May 1965. When I examined the whole position there I was very pleased to find that my staff had dealt with any remaining queries. In fact, I was able to get on with things as if I had never been away.

I arranged lodgings in Kentish Town. The practice was so busy that I felt I had to stay on longer than anticipated. When I talked to Breda and told her the position we agreed that for now I would become a more regular commuter. The next phone call I had from Breda was with some very good news – we would have another addition to our family in early 1966.

I still hoped that it would become easier to find a job in Ireland. If only I could, it would be much better to stay in Dublin with my family. While I was on a trip home to Ireland at about this time, July 1965, I was approached by a number of businessmen, mainly in the Waterford area, asking if I would consider taking on their accountancy and taxation work. In each case I advised them that I would think about it and let them know the position within a couple of weeks. I gave the matter some thought and decided that starting up a practice in Ireland just would not work.

My next trip to Dublin was on 10 August 1965. Meeting Breda and the kids again was great. I had made arrangements to spend a few weeks at home. We made plans to visit my parents on a couple of occasions and the time spent in Ireland flew by again.

Phone calls to my secretary in London became more urgent. Over a year already since we moved.

New cases continued to come in. I returned to London on 31 October 1965. Looking through the work files I was pleased to note that again we had got through everything successfully. This time I booked into a small hotel in Finsbury Park. Amongst the appointments made for me was one with a potential new client who had a relatively big business. I met him, got his business and spent a lot of time in his company.

My next trip home was on 23 September. The kids were developing well and going back to London was not getting any easier for me. I spent two weekends in Dublin during October, but then the office was so busy that my next trip home did not happen until 15 December. I stayed at home until just after the Christmas holidays. Then I returned to London on 3 January 1966, and worked in the practice until 20 January, when I returned to Dublin. Thinking about returning to my office was not easy. Breda went into the Coombe hospital and our second boy, Ian Patrick, was born on the 26 January 1966. During the period I was in Dublin I tried very hard again to get a job locally, but with no luck. I did get a couple of interviews and I was offered two jobs. One was as an accountant in a supermarket company's accounts department; the other was in an accountancy practice. Neither was well enough paid enough to cater for the family's needs.

Watching the two boys growing up alongside our girls was, of course, very special. I returned to London on 12 February to find that the practice was so busy that my next trip to Dublin (apart from two weekends in mid-February and early March) would be in late March. Appointments had been made for me with various clients, bank managers, tax inspectors and, of course, with new and potential clients. As well as football and other recreations I managed a couple of weekends in Dublin, which helped me to overcome the loneliness of my situation. I was looking forward to a three-week family holiday in August.

I relaxed during the first week. I hired a car and, as Ian was too young to go on a long holiday, we decided to do a number of day trips to the seaside, not too far from Dublin. This worked out quite well. But, as with holidays in the previous couple of years, the time went by far too quickly. After two years of our 'emigration' I was no nearer to moving back to Ireland. Not very satisfactory!

I started my third year of 'emigration' from my London office on 5 August 1966. My first job was to go through the appointments made for me by my secretary. One was with a potential client in a town in the midlands in England. Before I went to see this businessman, I had a few calls to make to existing clients and bank managers also one to an inspector of taxes. I dealt with all the local calls and then made a call to the taxpayer in the midlands. I learnt from him that he was a building contractor and that his turnover was higher than anything I had previously dealt with. I went to see him on 9 September, found out that he had a full time bookkeeper, a secretary and two clerks. His office was quite impressive. He mentioned a client of mine – my biggest client up to then – was a friend of his. He told me that I had been recommended to him. I took on the case.

This decision started a period in the practice which lifted it to a higher level. I had to spend more time in the area than anticipated. The reason for this was that a few other businesses, all Irish-owned, made appointments. I found out where the Irish community got together. In October 1966 I was staying at a hotel in Northampton and after a session of cards – the popular Irish game, '25' – I came up with the idea of a publication to bring the Irish communities together. I was thinking of either a periodical magazine or a weekly newspaper. It was something for consideration but not at the moment. Maybe in the New Year I would give it some more thought. I returned to London and set up the programme for my staff to cover up to the Christmas holidays and the month of January. Before my next trip to Dublin on 10 December I dealt with all the outstanding queries, phone calls and correspondence.

This time Christmas was a very sad one for all the family because, on 16 December, my mother died after a relatively short illness. She had been diagnosed with cancer in August of that year but her illness was too advanced to be treated successfully. It was very hard visiting her in hospital for the last time (although at the time I didn't know it would be my last time seeing her alive). She was always so unselfish. Her last words to me were, 'Be careful driving back to Dublin.' I was only back in Dublin when I got the sad news that she had passed away. Over the next couple of days my family made all the necessary arrangements and after Requiem Mass on 18 December my mother was laid to rest alongside her own mother in the graveyard at Newtown church, Kilmacthomas. It took us a long time to become reconciled to the fact that she would no longer be at home when we visited.

When I returned to my work in London in January 1967 I found that two meetings had been set up for me in Northampton. One was with the new client and the other was a case whose name was new to me. At least this type of meeting allowed me to concentrate on the business. I even took accounts to my hotel. I got home for Ian's first birthday. It was even more difficult leaving again to return to London. I didn't know how much longer I could carry on with this commuting. The snatched weekends were a bonus but the times away from the family were just getting more and more difficult. I even played some Gaelic football to pass some time in London. The business was growing all the time, but my thoughts were with the family.

I went home in August 1967 for my annual holiday. I hired a Mercedes and we went on a tour of part of Ireland. We travelled from Dublin to Wexford, then to Waterford, Cork and Kerry.

From there, after a few days, we went to Limerick, Galway and then back to Dublin. I returned to London in early September I continued to be very busy. I snatched a few weekends again in Dublin and before I realised it Christmas 1967 was upon us. It was obvious that we could not take any more. In early 1968, during one of our phone calls, Breda realised how concerned I was and suggested that the best way to sort out this problem was for the family to return permanently to London. We agreed that I would get on to estate agents the next day. I did and I arranged appointments to see houses. Breda flew over. As a result we bought a four-bedroomed detached house in Enfield, Middlesex. The whole procedure took only a few weeks and finally we moved into our new home. Ecstasy! When we moved to Ireland in 1964 we were a family of four. Now on our return we were a family of six.

Being with my family was wonderful. Breda and I went to the church to find out about the schools from Father Reynolds, the priest-in-charge. We then went to St George's primary school and enrolled Catherine and Claire as pupils. Paul and Ian were, of course, too young for school but we were able to enrol them at the convent nursery school. We were a complete family again, no more commuting to Ireland and I would see my children growing up. It felt really great – I was a very happy man.

6

THE CELTIC ERA

This story started on 1 March 1964 when a friend of mine who played for Aer Lingus in the Travel Trade League asked me to come along and watch them in action some Sunday when I had nothing else to do. I did go, little knowing that this would be the start of the most enjoyable few years that I ever spent with any club in my whole career, either playing or in administration. I knew that the team was not having a good season but I looked forward to watching them. However, my friend approached me outside the dressing rooms and told me that they did not have a full team and asked if I would line out with them. It was only a friendly match against a side called Martinko. I told him that I had no playing gear but if he could find some, I would be delighted to play. He asked for my size and disappeared into the dressing room. When he appeared again he told me that they had found some gear but no boots, only canvas shoes. The shorts were too tight but at least I was able to put them on. But the jersey fitted. With me, they had nine players. So the match started and I had a sort of a game.

The Aer Lingus players were, as I had been told, not very good. Even with a full side we would not have been able to make a good match of this friendly. But with only nine players against eleven we had no chance. It was never a proper test and at the end we deservedly lost 3–0. After a shower and change it was no surprise when a couple of club officers asked me if I would play in their five remaining league fixtures. I said I would think about it and let them know in a few days. After considering it and realising that I had no further commitments before the end of the season, I confirmed to them that I would help in the centre-forward position until the end of the season.

The standard was much poorer than I had anticipated but a promise is a promise! The first league match was against a team called Blue Cars on 22 March. I really enjoyed the match and fitted in a lot better than I expected. We won 4–2. As this was my first competitive match for the club, I can remember a few things about it. I scored two goals and laid on the other two. More than anything I can recall the ecstasy and celebration afterwards. Outsiders would think that the team had won the Cup. I realised that many of the players were not of a great standard but as I did not give any further consideration to the position, I thought that just by turning up for the few matches involved I would have fulfilled my promise. After a couple of approaches by the officers with a view to my taking over and running the club, I told them to get in touch with me in the close season and I would then make a decision. The next match on 19 April was against one of the strong league sides of the time, LEP Travel. The walkover that LEP expected did not take place. It was an excellent match which could have gone either way but in the end LEP were quite happy to take the two points at stake on the final scoreline of 5–3. Both sides really enjoyed it and the more experienced LEP side deserved to win.

The next week our opponents were Beejay. This time we continued our good form of the previous week and, believe it or not, we won by 4–1. We were beginning to look like a team at last. Our next match was against a very experienced Glolunn side, and, like most other teams in the competition, they expected an easy win. But it did not work out like that. This was a very exciting match with end-to-end play. Again it could have gone either way. But in the end, perhaps it was a slight superiority in experience that swung it in Glolunn's favour and they pipped us by 2–1. The final match of the 1963–4 season was against the very strong LEP Travel. They again beat us by 2–0. In the end, they proved that they wanted to win more than we did. I was quite happy with the way our side was developing and felt that if the side stayed together we must be in with a chance next season.

The committee made contact with me in the close season, as they had promised, to find out what I would do. I told them that I had decided to join them. I had no other recreational plans for 1964–5 so I decided that I would concentrate on this team. I signed on, was made captain and won the agreement that I could pick the team and bring in new players as the season developed. The idea of being fully in charge of the team – now renamed Celtic – was very exciting. Our first league opponents were the side that beat us twice last season – LEP. What a match! They won again by 4–3. We were not happy with that result. The committee expressed their pleasure at our performance but I made it quite clear that I was not. I started to make a few enquiries about the players I wanted and found out that I could have three of them in about three weeks. In the meantime we played our second league match. Our opponents were another of the league's strong sides, Worktrancy. This too was an excellent match which could have gone either way but, in the end, we lost by two goals to one. Worktrancy took their chances very well and their greater experience just pulled them through. I was pleased with the development of our side but, against that, we were joint bottom with no points from two matches. Not a good start but when my new players arrived things changed dramatically.

Over the next two months we played five matches. Our first was against Goodsons. Our performance was more like what I expected and we won by five goals to one. Our next match was against Inter. The good form continued and we had another excellent win by six goals to nil. Our next opponents were Amex. Co who had a reputation of being able but erratic. We just did not know what sort of team we could expect to meet. They were a useful side but we had no trouble and won comfortably 4–0. The next game was against the all-Italian side, Alitalia. We heard that, like us, they were trying to build up a useful side but obviously that had not happened yet. We had no problems with them and ran out easy winners by seven goals to one. Four wins in a row! Our next match was against another strong side, Global. It was an excellent game. Either side could have won. But this time we got the final break and won 2–1. For us, five wins in a row. Nobody in the club could remember such a run previously.

The *Travel Trade Gazette* Cup then intervened. We got a bye in the first round and in the quarter-final we were drawn against Alitalia. We expected a tough match but we were pleasantly surprised. From the start we were well on top and at the finish we won by six goals to nil. We even had a few spectators and, from the comments after the match, it seemed they would be back. Our next match was the cup semi-final. Our opponents were one of the league's strong sides – Guppy Transport. By now, we were also considered to be one of the strong sides. As is usual with a match where there are two good sides in opposition it is a matter of to-ing and fro-ing during the first quarter. Near half-time we took the lead deservedly, and led by that goal at half-time. They equalised early in the second half. But then we got well on top and scored two more goals. I scored all three of our goals and, with about six or seven minutes to go, and cruising at 3-1, I thought we were there.

An innocent punt by one of their players seemed to be going harmlessly wide. Our left-full-back thought that is was wide and stretched up to catch it and pass it on to our goalkeeper for the goal-kick. Unfortunately, our player was just inside the pitch and the penalty area when he caught the ball. The referee blew his whistle for a penalty. They scored. Now at 3–2 some of our players hung their heads, probably because of the way the penalty had been conceded. So it was no surprise when they equalised in the very last few seconds. Our bad run continued and after about five minutes of extra time Guppy Transport took the lead. A few minutes later one of our boys equalised 4–4. That was the half-time score. Again after a few minutes of the second half they went ahead 5–4. A few minutes to go and I equalised with my fourth goal of the match. I thought that with less than two minutes to go we would both be happy with a draw and a replay to come. No, with less than a minute to go they scored another goal which was the winner – six goals to five. To lose any cup semi-final is very disappointing but to score four goals and lose is something that would have to be experienced to be understood.

In the 1965–6 season I was more hopeful than confident that Celtic would end up at the top of the league table at the end of the season. We had to settle for being runners-up in the league championship and in the Travel Trade cup. Before the start of the 1966 season we decided to give the Travel Trade league one last shot. Win or lose, we felt that it would then be time for a new challenge. I was informed that a famous Gaelic footballer had arrived in London to do a university postgraduate course. His name was Martin Newell and he was one of the stars in Galway's team who had won three All-Ireland senior football titles in 1964, '65 and '66. I got in touch with him and told him all about Celtic football club and asked him if he would like to have a go with us. He said that he would be in London for twelve months and that he would enjoy getting involved with us as a player. Having heard a lot about his ability, I knew that we had a good signing. One or two other players who had heard about us applied for trials. But we took nobody else on. I was quite happy with our squad and looked forward to what should be an interesting season. As with the previous season there were ten teams in the league.

In all my playing years I had never, ever played in such a successful league team. But the season was not over yet. Celtic were still in the *Travel Trade Gazette* Cup. I missed the first two rounds due to an Achilles-tendon injury. But we won both matches with an aggregate of seven goals for and none against. This brought us into the semi-final. I was back in the side and playing well. Midway through the second half of this match, which took place on Hampstead Heath playing fields on a very damp day we were twelve goals to nil ahead. I had scored five of these goals. Every goal-scoring player likes to be able to say that he scored a double hat-trick (six goals) in a match and on this wet, muddy day I was all out to do that. Our right-winger was on his way with a good run. I ran in to connect with the expected cross ball. A beauty came across. As I went to head in my sixth goal a player behind me crashed into my back. I fell into the mud. Then I heard a voice behind me saying laughingly, 'You'd think we badly needed a goal.' I looked behind and laughed too. It was Martin Newell, who had also scored five goals. Before the end our team scored one more goal. We beat Constantine Social Club by thirteen goals to nil. What a way to win a cup semi-final!

Now for the final. We had scored twenty goals and conceded none in the cup. The match programme and the press cuttings show the position. In the final we won by two goals to nil, with goals from Martin Newell and myself. So the double which we had lost in 1965–6 was now ours. Two gold medals! For me and all my team-mates this was a wonderful season. But as we had nothing else to win in the Travel Trade League it was, we agreed, time to move on.

I made some enquiries and we applied to join the North London Sunday Football League. We were accepted and, although the league was aware of our previous achievements, they decided to place us in the second division for 1967–8. In the cup competitions we did very well and over the season I played a total of 20 matches and scored 18 goals. The 1968–9 season was essentially a write-off. I was too busy and for that and other reasons we decided unanimously to withdraw from the league. And so it went on; I enjoyed it hugely and, though I say it myself showing quite a record of success in playing and administration. We came top of the league in 1969–70, winning fourteen matches, drawing two and losing none!

Before the following 1970–1 season started, I formally told the Celtic club that I would no longer be available to play regular matches but that I would sign on and be available to play in emergencies – and, as I said at the time, it would have to be an emergency if I was called in. Celtic carried on, but I was no longer involved and ended by wishing them continued good luck and success. On reflection, although I had some good seasons throughout my 'career,' the whole period with Aer Lingus/Celtic was by far the most enjoyable.

7

THE *IRISH POST*

The *Irish Post* was born in a hotel in the English Midlands. My accountancy business was going through a particularly busy period between 1967 and 1969 and I virtually lived out of a suitcase as my hectic schedule took me to all corners of the UK. During these travels I would meet members of the Irish community in various clubs and haunts, and it became very clear to me that they had no means of communicating with Irish groups in other towns. The Irish of Nottingham, for instance, knew nothing of their counterparts in Newcastle. The Coventry Irish were strangers to their soulmates in Cardiff and there was no bond between Willesden and Walsall.

The logical way to reach them seemed to be a newspaper or magazine: a national organ and information sheet dedicated solely to the welfare of the Irish community in Britain and to furthering their cause. Ideally, it should be run by an experienced team of Irish journalists with a fellow-countryman at the helm. Like Topsy the idea grew and I started to look for a professional newspaperman who fitted the bill but was unsuccessful in locating the right person among the ranks of the expatriate community.

Eventually I found Brendan Mac Lua, who had a publishing background in Ireland and I persuaded him to join me in the venture. We worked tirelessly side-by-side formulating the style and content of my new baby and so jointly founded the *Irish Post*. As an accountant I realised that like any new business the project would have cashflow problems for the first twelve months or so, and it was therefore necessary to make arrangements for an overdraft facility. In those days banks weren't queuing up to lend you money as they are today; they were reluctant to advance money or underwrite anything which wasn't a rock-bottomed certainty. However being in the money business, I had a few useful contacts to help get the idea off the ground and also to provide a financial cushion against any unforeseen difficulties which might arise in the first twelve months or so.

That was really the easy part compared to the time and effort I had to put in during the immediate pre-launch period and the first few months of publication. I was still running the accountancy business full-time, and at the end of each normal working day (Monday and Tuesday) I would drive to the printers in Slough to proofread the editorial content. Then there would be time spent interviewing potential staff and making visits to various Irish organisations to bang the drum for the idea. Later I would become enmeshed in a myriad social events where, as chairman of the *Irish Post*, I was expected to make a speech or a presentation. In those economically uncertain times I found it difficult to sleep at night for worrying whether my dream of the *Irish Post* would take off or collapse around me.

We had appointed Pat Chatten, an experienced Irish journalist, as our first editor and in order to attract potential advertisers we produced our first dummy issue in December 1969. I was relieved to find that it had generated a high level of interest among the Irish financial and industrial corporations. The tourist industry supported us too and we soon had comments from Ryans, B & I Line, Murphy's the builders and the Irish TGWU. To cap this, both main Irish banks bought a whole page of advertising. We decided to fly in the face of superstition by launching the *Irish*

Post on Friday 13 February 1970. We felt we were big enough to overcome any bad ju-ju and, in retrospect, it proved to be a lucky day for us. There was plenty of interest in the inaugural issue but this was only to be expected. People were inquisitive and bought it for its novelty value, much as they have done with the handful of new national daily and Sunday newspapers which have been launched in recent years.

I often thumb through that first issue. The lead story picked the bones out of a speech made at our inaugural luncheon by the late George Colley, Irish Minister for Industry and Commerce, who made an impassioned plea for the Irish in Britain to use their voting power to support candidates who sympathised with the Irish viewpoint. Other issues covered included the outburst from Enoch Powell, then MP for Wolverhampton, who said that his party would ensure that the Irish would have no preference entering Britain, and should expect the same treatment as the French. Russians and Australians. A random survey showed that the Irish were three to one in favour of returning home if they could find a job with similar pay and conditions. There was also an exclusive interview with Con Murphy, chairman of the advisory committee for services to immigrants who wished to return home.

A new Irish centre had just opened in Leeds and the Liverpool equivalent was celebrating its fifth anniversary. There was a round-up of provincial news from Ireland, a women's page, a show-business page and a profile of Johnny Giles of Leeds United and Ireland, certainly one of the sporting heroes of the time. For advocates of the other variety of football, there was an extensive preview of the match between England and Ireland at Twickenham the following day and all this for an old-fashioned shilling! We printed 84,000 copies of the first issue but, in my time there, we never reached that figure again.

As I have said, the initial reaction was encouraging, but

my concern was to ensure that both readers and advertisers would stick with it and I embarked on a lengthy programme of promotional visits to Irish clubs and centres, not just to sell the paper but also to sell its *concept*. I had to answer countless questions on editorial policy and gradually it became clear to the much-maligned and often-rejected Irish community in Britain that they had a champion, an ally on whom they could rely. People started to write letters, airing their views on controversial issues. Other readers reacted and this spawned more correspondence making the letters page an open forum for diverse points of view on anything that breathed, moved or perhaps more pertinently, occupied a parliamentary seat. I can still recall, in those early days, the pride I felt just seeing the paper in newsagents in all parts of Britain. It was sold in Ireland too, for many emigrants returned to their homeland in the 1970s and wanted to keep up with news of their colleagues in Britain.

It was important that we indicate our stance on a wide variety of topical and controversial issues affecting the Irish community. First of all, we refused to be neatly categorised. We also wanted to retain the facility to communicate with the great mass of Irish people in Britain. Major points in our manifesto included our views on jobs: we provided practical information on employment opportunities in Ireland and helped to create more work by the promotion of Irish goods and services to Britain; on the reunification of Ireland we pointed out that in the unlikely event of this happening in the immediate future, the vast majority of Irish emigrants would have to remain in Britain and it would be the duty of the *Irish Post* to safeguard the interests and welfare of these people; on emigration we emphasised that half the people of Ireland were living in Britain because their own country couldn't accommodate them. We pointed out that successive Irish governments had done damn all for the welfare of the Irish in Britain, and that the *Irish Post* would not be guilty of this oversight. We further stated that the Irish in Britain could not be blamed should they choose to revoke all commitment to their home country which had first spurned them and then become virtually oblivious of them.

Fortunately, the emigrant community has chosen to nurture its roots rather than sever them, and Irish culture, particularly dancing, is more popular in Britain than it is in Ireland. Perhaps, in clinging to their roots, they are less likely to feel that they have been rejected by the land of their birth. Ireland has many champions and may it always have them but aren't the half who have opted to live in Britain entitled to have one champion who will put their interest above all other things? This was the role to which the *Irish Post* committed itself from the start. Its banner head said: 'A voice for the Irish in Britain' and nothing changed during my period as co-proprietor of the newspaper.

Those early days of the *Irish Post* marked probably the most hectic period I can recall. My life assumed a lunatic pace as I endeavoured to attend Irish functions in Portsmouth, Leeds, Coventry, Liverpool, Harlow, Maidenhead and all over London – wherever the Irish were seen to assemble, Beatty would be there to attend dinners, make speeches and present awards. On top of this, there was the endless round of business lunches with potential advertisers. Being a committed member of the Pioneer Total Abstinence Association, I would find these sessions something of a drag but it was business so I knew I had no alternative but to bite on the bullet and suffer through their white wine, red wine, port and brandy. In addition to these business-cum-social commitments, I would also have to read editorial proofs at the printers in Slough a couple of evenings a week. Then we would collect some of the papers from the printers, bind them up and put them on trains or special delivery vehicles to ensure distribution. The professional distributors dealt with most of this work. And, oh yes, I still had an accountancy business to run!

They were busy times, but this level of effort and dedication was necessary if we were to build a strong foundation for the newspaper. Perhaps my main regret was the fact that many of these events accounted for a large part of the weekends when, like most men, I would have cherished more time with my wife and family. The timetable for a typical Saturday was accountancy in the morning, a brief lunch at home, then off to catch a train to the evening destination which could be anywhere from Cornwall to Cumbria. I would then catch an hour's sleep before changing into my dinner jacket and preparing myself for a lengthy dinner followed by drinks and speeches. I was never allowed to crash out on my bed until the early hours of the following morning. And then I would have to be up with the first sparrows to catch an early train home and salvage what was left of the weekend. Thank God, I was fit in those days for the schedule was tough but as the saying goes 'when the going gets tough, the tough get going'.

One of the most enjoyable and rewarding functions I have ever had to perform, was the official opening of the Irish centre in Leeds in June 1970. The event generated much local interest and I was impressed to see television cameras present. Then it dawned on me that they would be filming the actual opening ceremony, including my speech, and for the first time in my public life I felt truly terrified. I somehow staggered through the opening address, trying hard not to allow my attention to be distracted by the TV cameras or the myriad flashlight bulbs that kept popping at me. By the time my ordeal was over I must have shed half a pound of sweat, terrified that half the Yorkshire TV area would be exposed to the inane ramblings of a retarded Irishman who had suddenly landed in their midst. My fears proved totally unfounded and when I saw the programme a few hours later. I couldn't believe how cool I looked, the complete professional who did this sort of thing every day of his life, a man who was clearly in control of the situation. If only they knew. I often wonder how I would behave in similar circumstances if I drank alcohol, which tends to flow in abundance at this type of event. Fortunately it has never interested me but I know that the many who rely on it to calm their nerves at public appearances are never in full command of the situation and often allow the odd *mal mot* to slip out.

The Irish are a great nation for champions. We love nothing more than seeing one of our own rise to the pinnacle of his or her career. Perhaps it is because history has given us so relatively few successes to celebrate, that we enjoy it all the more when it happens, and when it does we acclaim our champion with genuine delight. It was for this reason that we decided that the *Irish Post* should run an annual competition for 'Irish Personality of the Year'. Readers were invited to submit nominations from which a shortlist would be drawn and it was then up to the readers to vote for the personality of their choice. Then the fun would start. Once the winners had been decided, it was my job to contact either them or their families to determine a suitable date and venue for the presentation. In order to get some meat for the presentation speech, we had to dig into their background, which gave a tremendous insight into the sort of problems encountered by researchers for personality programmes like *This Is Your Life*. By the time we had enough material, we felt we knew the winner like one of our own family. Like most competitions, there was only one winner while there were several losers but it was all good fun and I felt very proud at each presentation I made.

Apart from politicians, charity workers and other social heroes, there was the anticipated glut of nominations from the world of sport and it wasn't long before we decided to run a separate poll for sportsmen, past and present. This blossomed into two awards, 'Sportsman of the Year' and 'Sports Star of the Past', and sporting giants who were honoured in this way included Pat Jennings, Liam Brady, Jonjo O'Neill, Tommy Stack, Johnny Carey. Peter Doherty, Alex Higgins, Denis Taylor, Pat Eddery, Walter

Swinburn, Danny McAlinden and, of course, the man we chose to feature in our first issue, Johnny Giles. While we tried to ensure that these presentations were made at dinners or other social gatherings, it hadn't always been possible and we've experienced a variety of venues. The presentation to Johnny Giles was made in the middle of the Leeds United pitch at Elland Road, while Steve Heighway received his accolade before an international match in Copenhagen. (Being a soccer fan myself I considered these locations to be a bonus!) On the other hand, there was the odd location at which I felt like a fish out of water. The award to Frank Canning at his pub in County Galway is one that readily springs to mind, and another instance where wine flowed liberally in all directions but mine, was the presentation to Mickey Walsh made in a London restaurant. But it doesn't matter. At all times I felt it was a privilege to he in the company of men and women who had reached the pinnacle of sporting achievement, all the more so because not too many years earlier, I had nurtured secret ambitions of a future as a professional sportsman.

Sport was a high editorial priority in those early days and, naturally, I took a keen interest. Rarely would a Sunday go by without a visit to the Gaelic Athletic Grounds at New Eltham, where they had three pitches with two or three matches being played on each pitch. The surface took a hammering, but it illustrates the level of interest in Gaelic games among the expatriate community, most of whom had been reared on a diet of Gaelic football and hurling. I had for some time been thinking about inviting a top international player to write a specialist soccer column for the paper and I was now convinced that, if the rest of my countrymen shared my sports fever, it would go down well with the readers.

One of my greatest friends in the sporting world was Jimmy Conway, Republic of Ireland international winger. He was playing with Fulham in the early 1970s when I invited him to

Tony's paternal grandmother, Ellen, who was born in America.
Tony never met her.

Tony's paternal grandfather, Barney, outside his house in Abbeyside, Dungarvan,
with his daughter (Tony's aunt Lil) in the early 1940s

Tony, early 1947

Tony, aged about six months,
in his father's arms, early 1936

Tony's uncle Tommy, grandmother Katherine, aunt Kathleen and uncle Paty
with Tony in his arms, aged about eighteen months, in early 1937

Tony, fourth from right, middle row
Currabaha Boys' National School, Kilmacthomas, late 1947

Tony's mother and three of his sisters, 1949
Left to right (back): Eileen, Tony's mother, Mary. Patsy is in front.

Tony's elder daughter, Catherine, on his father's postman's bicycle, 1967

Tony and his sister Mary, early 1950s

Kilamacthomas, County Waterford

The all-conquering Celtic team, 1966-7

Mícheál O'Hehir and Tony at a
charity golf day, 1980s

Irish Post star Steve Heighway is presented with his award by
David O'Leary in Copenhagen on the occasion of
an Ireland away match in 1978. Tony is in the background.

Tony with Barry McGuigan at the
Irish Post awards, early 1980s

Pat Jennings and Tony at one of the
Irish Post awards days, 1988

Tony and Bob Geldof at the *Irish Post* community awards, 1980s

Tony introducing Cardinal Hume and Ambassador Kennedy
at the Irish Centre, 1980s

Tony presenting Frank Stapleton with his Sportsman of the Year award, 1980s

The day Tony received his Pope's Award medal, October 1988

Tony with his son Ian on their way to the *Irish Post* awards ceremony, 1995. Ian accepted an award on behalf of his sister, Catherine, who was unable to attend

Stars to Killmac, 1977: Back row: Tony (first on left); Ireland's David O'Leary (fourth from left); goalkeeper Wales's Martin New (fifth from left); Ireland's Frank Stapleton (fifth from right); England's Graham Rix (third from right); Front row: Ireland's Jimmy Conway (sixth from left): Ireland's David Langan (fourth from right)

contribute his own soccer column. He jumped at the chance, and the *Conway Column* became a widely-read and successful feature of the sports section. Later, Jimmy moved to Manchester City but he continued to subscribe to the editorial content until he signed for Portland Timbers in Oregon, USA. This move precluded him from continuing to write regularly on Irish soccer matters but I was delighted that he kept in touch both with myself and with the newspaper and continued to write the occasional piece for us.

Having such close ties with many soccer stars, and being keen about the game myself, at that time it was perhaps inevitable that I should start to support actively the national team, and I soon became one of the band of regular fans who would travel anywhere to see their beloved 'green shirts' play soccer. Not much chance of a win though, for in those days the Irish were traditionally strong at home but pretty much a walkover when they were playing away. I am delighted to say that this is no longer the case, and nothing has given me greater pleasure than to see the renaissance of Irish soccer in the past few years under the guidance of an Englishman, Jack Charlton, culminating in their richly-deserved success in the World Cups in Italy in the summer of 1990 and in America in 1994. In the 2002 World Cup, under manager Mick McCarthy, they came through a very tough group to qualify for the Japan and Korea finals.

An Irish trip that looms large in the memory, although for completely different reasons, was the Irish match against USSR in Kiev in 1975. The game was to be played on a Sunday afternoon so, like the good Catholics we are (even if a little naive) our priority in the morning was to attend Mass. Alas, there was no Catholic church but fortunately there was a soccer-loving priest among our number. When I was about eight years of age, a few of my friends – John Foley, Dick Prendergast, Billy Baldwin and Patsy Walsh – started training to be altar servers. When they were studying for a few months they were nearly ready to start.

I started later than the others but I was not getting on as well as I felt that I should. In the end, I gave up. When the Latin was replaced by English it was much easier but it was also too late for me. Anyway in Kiev the priest, showing admirable presence of mind, succeeded in requisitioning a local restaurant which he converted for the purpose. I was coopted to help him to put tables together to make an altar and, although it was a great match in the afternoon, my abiding memory is not of the game (which we lost by 2-1) but of helping the priest to celebrate Mass in a restaurant which, only a few hours earlier had been full of Saturday-night revellers eating and no doubt knocking back the kirsch and the vodka!

Another thing happened that day – something I will never forget. The attendance at the match was very large and noisy but at the start, as in all international fixtures, the national anthems were played. Apart from the team, there were hardly a couple of dozen Irish fans amongst the tens of thousands of noisy Russians. Then it was time for our anthem, '*Amrán na bhFiann*' ('The Soldiers' Song'). The noise stopped and you could almost hear a pin drop with the respect shown by the large attendance. What a moment of pride when we stood alongside one of the most powerful nations in the world – as equals. My last trip with the Irish soccer squad was to Japan in 1984 for the Japan Cup tournament. Breda came with me and we had a wonderful three-week holiday. Doing reports and organising a photographer in Japan to get a photo of the first ever Republic team to reach a senior final gave me a lot of pleasure.

In addition to helping develop the sports coverage of the *Irish Post*, I took a close look at the news and feature content of the paper and decided we needed more emphasis on local leisure activities. I embarked on a programme of research which took me to numerous pubs and clubs throughout the UK where the Irish gather for their *fleánna ceoil* or cultural evenings. Here, they would hold Irish language classes, organise sporting events and promotions and attend quiz evenings in much the same way as many British pub devotees do today. The one difference was the involvement of the Catholic Church in these evenings, often in fundraising events to finance major structural repairs or help towards the numerous activities that had been conceived and developed under its influence. The Church benefited greatly from these gatherings for, while the Irish are traditionally not a wealthy race, I know them to be among the most generous people in the world. News of these events was welcomed and the resulting exchange of ideas between towns and cities did much to bring the Irish community in Britain closer together. I was delighted on more than one occasion to hear the *Irish Post* referred to as a sophisticated parish newsletter, not quite the sort of comment that your average newspaper proprietor would want to hear, I'm sure, but for me it hit the spot. It meant that we were achieving exactly what we had set out to do.

It was certainly a busy period of my life, perhaps the most hectic I have ever experienced, with the endless roundabout of official evening and weekend functions, proofreading, deliveries and meetings. No wonder I was amused, and not a little hurt, to hear someone say many years later that Beatty never did any work for the paper! As the years went by I was to discover that I would have worse allegations levelled against me. Is this a penalty of success? On top of this, my personal life was torn to shreds by a number of deeply wounding tragedies.

In my years as chairman I was involved in many interesting events. I now propose to share some of them with you. On launch day there was an unforeseen problem. The Irish flag was flown. However, protocol required that the Union Jack should fly alongside it and none could be found Finally, after a few frantic phone calls the local British Legion club in Stoke Road, Slough, came to our rescue. In the early days of the paper we, like all commercial publications, required advertising personnel and I found a man who remained an employee of the paper for many years. I refer to Pat Conway, and this is how I came to find him. My accountancy office took various professional magazines and in the advertising section of one such publication I saw Pat's name. When I phoned up and talked to him I found out about his Irish connections. He left his job and we took him on. He spent many years with us as a loyal and valued employee of the paper.

On Saturday, 27 June 1970 I attended a most enjoyable function. I was invited to do the official opening of the fête at St Joseph's School, Maidenhead. I was not sure what to expect but it turned into a wonderful occasion. Breda and our four children were with me. We were welcomed by Canon Murtagh on behalf of the school. He then introduced me to the large crowd who turned up to support the event. Then it was my turn. First of all I realised that many of the people among the very large attendance had never heard of the *Irish Post* so, in my speech, I gave them an indication of what it was and what it would be. Many people probably thought, 'A waste of space. Why does he not say something sensible'? *C'est la vie!*

When I performed the official opening of the Leeds Irish centre on Monday, 8 June 1970, the address which I gave is as relevant to any Irish club today as it was then. Some of the points I made were:

> I look on the gesture extended to me to be much more a recognition of *The Irish Post* and what it represents, than it is to me. The Irish centre in Leeds and the *Irish Post* are about the same thing. They are about the Irish in Britain coming into their own and not being bashful about it. They mean that we, the Irish community in Britain, recognise some degree of permanency in our stay here and are taking steps

to ensure that, while we are here, we will not abandon our own Irish individuality and traditions. The Leeds Irish centre is a monument to the enterprise and foresight of those in Leeds who conceived the idea. In providing it, the Leeds Irish community is showing what can be achieved when people with the right motivation firmly set themselves a task. The centre means that Leeds has a united and vibrant Irish community which, standing together, can achieve almost anything practical it desires. Without the centre there would be an insignificant scattering of Irish people devoid of a voice or ethnic purpose. Sincere congratulations are due to everybody who had a hand in bringing this achievement.

The Portsmouth Irish Society's contribution to the Irish in Britain is so vast that a whole book could be written about it. In March 1971, the Portsmouth Irish Society and its leaders, Jim Kirby, Bill Halley and Jack Griffin were so important to the Irish community in Britain that I have decided to reproduce in full the article that I wrote for the programme of the centre's Irish Week in 1971:

What it means: I deem it a great honour to be asked to open the Portsmouth Irish Week and, in doing so, to be associated with those who have, through it, contributed so much to the Irish community in Britain.

The Portsmouth Irish Society was founded in 1949 and from it came, in 1952, the first Portsmouth Irish Week. This society and that event was to provide the basis for what is now the Federation of Irish Societies – easily the most significant Irish organisation in Britain today.

The people who founded the Portsmouth Irish Society almost twenty-two years ago are now the leaders of the Federation of Irish Societies and this is as it should be, for it is their foresight and vision which has been responsible for the development all over Britain of the fine centres which are now the focal points of Irish community life in this country.

From Portsmouth and from the Portsmouth Irish Society has come a new approach to Irish life in Britain. It is an approach which facilitates the full integration of the immigrant Irish while at the same time seeking to retain all of their own cultural and historical values.

In addition, the Portsmouth style has been one of uplifting the Irish community in its social habits and meeting places. As such, the contribution made by those who founded the Portsmouth Irish Society and who now present Portsmouth Irish Week 1971, has been enormous. The extent of this Portsmouth contribution has yet to be fully realised but it will be in time and then it will be seen as the single factor which most brought about the contented and progressive Irish community which we have in Britain today.

It is for these reasons that I am very proud to be associated with Portsmouth Irish Week 1971 and with the officers and members of the Portsmouth Irish Society.

I had another very interesting duty to attend to in Portsmouth that evening. The election of the Irish Person of the Year had taken place and, fittingly, the winner was Jim Kirby of

Portsmouth. It gave me great pleasure to make the presentation to him.

An invitation to the South London Irish Association annual dinner and dance at he Waldorf Hotel, Aldwych, London on Friday, 20 October 1971 was interesting in so far as it was their *third* annual function, which meant that it had started in 1969 – the year before the *Irish Post* was founded. Talking to people (mainly fellow immigrants) it was very interesting to find out why such organisations as this one emerged. It also confirmed to me why my idea for a paper like the *Irish Post* became so successful. Incidentally, my speech at this function was a response on behalf of the guests. Two years later I was also invited as guest to that association's fifth annual dinner dance on Friday, 16 March 1973, at the Shannon Suite, London Tara Hotel. I was also asked to respond on behalf of the guests at this function.

Every few years the Irish ambassador is changed. During my term with the paper there were several changes of personnel. From the beginning, each ambassador was most supportive and helped with presentations and in any other way he could. Every year there is a traditional pre-St Patrick's Day reception given by the embassy which is attended by over 200 representatives of Irish community organisations in London. In 1973 the ambassador was Dr Donal O'Sullivan who, like his predecessors, got involved with and helped the Irish community when he could. As a tribute to his efforts, he was elected Irish Person of the Year in Britain. It was my most enjoyable task to present him with his award. To tidy things up his wife was not forgotten and she was presented with a bouquet. In 1974 the award went to Tom Walsh of the Liverpool Irish Centre. In 1975 it was Johnny Giles's turn, because of his work in the development of the Ireland soccer team.

The 1975 award was touchingly different. It was presented posthumously to the family of the late Nurse Nuala Woods at a private function in the London Tara Hotel. Nuala Woods, a native of Ballyconnell, County Cavan, died in a London nursing-home fire in August 1975. Having led most of her patients from the blazing building she went back in through the smoke and flames in a heroic effort to rescue two remaining old ladies. She died with them. She was twenty-eight years old. The readers of *The Irish Post* voted her Irish Person of the Year in Brtain: the first woman to be chosen and the first person to win the award posthumously. Her mother, Mrs Maureen Woods, travelled from Ireland to accept the award – a specially designed plaque bearing the Woods family crest and a brief note recalling the circumstances. I was proud and privileged to be the person, as chairman of the *Irish Post*, to make that presentation. Nuala Woods's brother Noel replied on behalf of the family and said that they were very moved by the tribute paid to their sister. In addition to being a tribute to her, the Woods family, he said, interpreted the award as recogniton of the thousands of Irish nurses in Britain who over the years have devoted their lives to their profession.

My father used to get two English Sunday papers each week – the *Sunday Dispatch*, which he got from the local newsagent and the *News of the World*. This was passed on to him by a friend who received it each week by post from a relative in England. The back pages had all the soccer results from the English and Scottish leagues. As a curious ten-year-old I loved to read the sports pages. When I understood very basically what was going on and saw team names, players names and scores, plus Irish names – one name began to come up fairly often. That name was Peter Doherty. He played for Derby County, which seemed to be doing well in a cup competition. More news came forward about Peter Doherty. He was from Derry and played international football for Northern Ireland. He was my first international star and when Derby County won the FA Cup in 1946 I thought that it was because they had Peter Doherty on their team. For many years years after that he was remembered as an Irish superstar.

In those days hurling and Gaelic football were my games. Then in 1947 another name started to become familiar. That was Jackie (Johnny) Carey of Manchester United. The name of J. Carey seemed to be coming up more and more. When I found out that he was chosen in a European XI and that he was the Irish team captain, I knew that I would have to pursue that name and find out everything I could about him. Not alone was he in the Manchester United team that won the FA Cup in 1948 but he was captain. It is obvious why I looked up to those two players and treated them as heroes.

In those days there was no *Irish Post*. So you might wonder about the relevance of those names to the paper. When I realised that they qualified as 'sports stars of the past' I knew that those two men were ideal candidates. My dreams finally came true in 1976 when I presented Johnny Carey with his award and then in 1977 I presented Peter Doherty with his award.

Sometimes when an awardwinner could not for some reason attend the usual function arranged in London for presentations, I made other arrangements. In 1978 the famous Liverpool and Ireland player, Steve Heighway, was unable to travel to London for the presentation night. He was in Lisbon that night playing with Liverpool against Benfica. However, on the night David O'Leary who, at that time, was the soccer columnist for the paper, stood in for Steve. David looked after the award until an appropriate time arrived. It happened in, of all places, Copenhagen, where Ireland were playing Denmark in the European Nations Cup. I travelled with the Irish squad and, after speaking to David, arranged for a local photographer to be present when David handed over the award at a small ceremony in the courtyard of the Irish team's hotel. So it really was fitting that Steve received his International Performer Award at an international venue. Incidentally, the Denmark v. Republic of Ireland match was a thriller and ended in a high-scoring draw.

A unique and wonderful presentation evening was held at the Portman Hotel, London in March 1979. Since the inception of these functions shortly after the birth of the *Irish Post* there had never been such a gathering of stars. Recipients for this year included a number of players who, although born outside the country, declared for Ireland, through family backgrounds. Those players were David O'Leary, Mick Kearns, Gerry Peyton, Mark Lawrenson, Mickey Walsh, Brendan O'Callaghan and Tony Grealish. They each received an inscribed silver salver (International Award). Then it was the turn of the Footballer of the Year to receive his award. Martin O'Neill, from County Derry whose club at that time was Nottingham Forest, was the winner after many outstanding performances for his clubs and for his country, Northern Ireland. The top award was for Irish Sportsman of the Year. Because of the number of people who were involved as that year's winners, it was necessary to change the title from 'Irish Sportsman of the Year' to 'Irish Sportsmen of the Year.'

The Beech Hill Blues tug-of-war team from Luton, all thirteen members, were the 'Sportstars of the Year in Britain' for 1978. They had a clean sweep which earned them a place in the *Guinness Book of Records*. In addition to winning all the major titles in Britain, including the British AAA and the championship of England, they then crowned this year by winning the championship of the world. Tug-of-war may be a minority sport but Irishmen as world champions are always special. So it was that the thirteen men who comprised the Beech Hill Blues were deservedly honoured and it gave me great pleasure to make the presentations individually to each member.

Over the years it was my pleasure and privilege to present awards to a rich variety of Irish sports stars. In 1980 it was Micky Walsh, in '81 Frank Canning. Pat Jennings was honoured in 1982. In 1986 the world snooker title was won by Dennis Taylor; there was no doubt about who was the Irish sports star that year.

After the paper started in 1970 Breda and I were invited to many county associations annual dinner dances. The first invitation was from the London Mayo Association, and for many years after we looked forward to that function. Each year I was asked to make a speech, usually either to propose or respond to 'The Mayo Association' or to respond on behalf of the guests. This is the response I made on behalf of 'The Mayo Association' in 1975:

Since being asked to respond on behalf of the Mayo Association, I have been trying to figure out how a Waterford man could reply. Of course, it may seem unusual but the more I thought about it, the easier it seemed. After all, in context, Waterford is not far from Mayo. Bear in mind that the whole island of Ireland would fit many times into an American state – for example Texas – and we have too many divisions in our country.

Down the years, Mayo has been to the forefront in Irish affairs. This is the county that produced, for example, Michael Davitt, of Land League fame, Gráinne Ní Mhaoil, Major John MacBride, the famous 1916 man. And, of course, in Gaelic football circles, today's [late 70s] household names are people like Pat Spillane, Ogie Moran and Ger Power of Kerry but, just about thirty years ago, before some of those men were born, in 1950 and 1951, the big names were people like Padraig Carney, Tom Langan and Paddy Prendergast of Mayo. How times change!

On a personal point, I would like to place on record that, back in 1970, in the first year of the *Irish Post*, the Mayo Association in London was the first county association to extend a formal invitation to my wife and me to attend their annual dinner. We were delighted to accept and, over the years, we have spent some very enjoyable evenings at many Mayo dinners. Please accept our thanks.

Finally, the smaller attendances at these functions over the past few years can, I feel, be put down totally to the economic state of affairs. If there are any Mayo people here tonight who are not members of the association and would like to join, please see one of the officers.

This gives an indication of the type of speech required. I made many friends during those years and it naturally followed that in some years in the 1980s the Waterford golfing society, which I captained, had some really enjoyable matches against the Mayo golfing society, captained by Oliver Foy.

A few years later, in 1984, I was very pleased to receive an invitation from the Mayo county association in Birmingham to their silver jubilee dinner dance at the Albany Hotel, Birmingham held on 18 February. As usual, it was a most enjoyable night. My toast was 'The Mayo County Association.' As this was, for me, a one-off of which I was very proud, I have decided to give my speech in full:

> Friends – that covers everybody! The silver jubilee of any association is special. Tonight we celebrate the silver jubilee of the Mayo Association here. In doing so we recall that the county associations grew from the need for mutual help for emigrants settling in an unknown land where difficulties with jobs and accommodation posed big problems. Such associations were also needed to look

after the human and spiritual needs of the new emigrants and while functions such as this can be reported, the countless acts of kindness and help to individuals over the past twenty-five years are too numerous to chronicle. Imagine the early days of the association in the late 1950s – a young person emigrating from Mayo due to lack of work at home. On arriving in Birmingham that person found the Mayo Association, made up of like-minded people, ready and willing to help. Because of the confidence instilled and the skills and talents developed, Mayo people have reached the forefront of their adopted community. As a direct result, the Irish in Britain have been able to help the home economy, particularly in terms of tourism and remittances home.

It is sometimes said that the work of the county associations is finished. Rubbish! There is never an end to mutual help and the strength we receive from our roots and from the people who share our culture and outlook.

I now ask you to be upstanding for the toast: The Mayo County Association.

8

STARS TO KILMAC 1976–8

During the period when Jimmy Conway played for Fulham and contributed a weekly soccer column to the *Irish Post* he and I became quite friendly. He used to call to my accountancy office after football training on a couple of afternoons each week to get an indication of how a small business operated. I was quite pleased with his progress. At this time I went to many matches at Craven Cottage, Fulham's ground in West London with my two boys, Paul and Ian. Jimmy always got us three tickets to the special seats in the Cottage where the players from both teams met after the match. Before the match we had lunch in the restaurant under the main stand and when Fulham reached the FA cup final at Wembley in 1975, all three of us were there to support Jimmy and his team-mates. Unfortunately they lost the final to another London side, West Ham United. But it was a memorable occasion. During one of our regular meetings I told Jimmy about Kilmacthomas AFC, the club which I had helped to found and the forthcoming silver jubilee of the club. His response was excellent: 'If you think that there is any way that I can help, let me know.' When we talked in December 1975 he told me that he had decided what could be done but he would not give me any details until the next month. I decided not to mention anything to the lads at home until I had more specific information.

My meeting with Jimmy Conway about the Kilmac project took place on 10 January 1976. He got to the point straight away: 'Tony,' he said 'after considering the position, I spoke to my friend, David O'Leary of Arsenal. We have decided that if you can ask the club in Kilmac to set up some form of exhibition match for a date in the middle of June, we will both take part. Let me know as soon as possible.' I got on to Roy Battye, my friend in Kilmac, and told him the good news. He could not believe what he heard and said that a committee meeting would be arranged to first of all absorb the news and set a detailed plan of what will happen. Two days later Roy got in touch. He told me that everything was arranged: the match would be an exhibition, Past and Present, at the home venue, Alaska Park. After the match there would be a buffet and cabaret at the popular local venue Danny's. This is Kirwan's hostelry, now run by Danny Kirwan, son of the man who had helped to found the club – the late Mr Percy Kirwan.

The local papers did not give any preview coverage, giving the impression that they did not believe that star footballers would go to a small village to take part in a match to celebrate a club's milestone anniversary. One local paper, the *Waterford News and Star*, sent a reporter and photographer, as they said during the evening 'just in case those stars turned up'. The two stars enjoyed the function so much that they indicated they would come again in 1977 and bring some of their friends.

The Star did a good report, including photographs of the two teams. The report read:

> *A Night to Remember in Kilmac*
> *Present XI: 2–Past XI: 1*
> A night to remember is an apt description of the proceedings at Currabaha Park, Kilmacthomas, on Friday last when the local Soccer Club celebrated their 25th year of existence with the annual game

between teams representing the past and present generations of club members.

There was the usual big attendance and on this occasion the proceedings were made memorable by the attendance of Irish international players, Jimmy Conway (Fulham) and David O'Leary (Arsenal). The former togged out with the 'Past', with the young Arsenal star taking control of the whistle.

Both players attended at the invitation of Mr Tony Beatty, the well-known Kilmac native who is now a successful businessman in London. Mr Beatty, who togged out with the Past XI, invited the two Ireland players to mark the occasion of the club's 25th birthday.

Good Start

The Present team got off to a good start when Pat Mears scored a fine goal. Later the Past team came more into the game, with John O'Byrne and Jimmy Conway commanding midfield. The half-time whistle came with the Present team leading 1–0.

The second half saw some great football from both sides with the Past team scoring the equaliser with ten minutes remaining. And what a goal it was! John O'Byrne passed to Don Casey, who sent Jimmy Conway through and from thirty yards out he fired a great shot to the corner of the net go give Eamonn Lalor no chance.

The Winner

But with the last kick of the game, 16-year old Raymond Carey got the all-important winner. Present team won by two goals to one.

After the game teams and supporters went to Danny Kirwan's for the presentation of trophies and a jolly evening was had by all.

The Kilmacthomas Club thanked Allied Irish Banks who sponsored some beautiful trophies for the winners and runners-up – a very nice gesture indeed, which made it a night to remember in Kilmac.

Early in the following (1976–7) season I got in touch with the lads in the club at home and told them that a few of the players known to me had indicated that they had heard such good stories about the 1976 event they would like to attend as players for the 1977 event. At this stage, before Christmas, I told them that I would finalise all arrangements in January. The following players had agreed to travel from Arsenal: David O'Leary, Graham Rix, Martin New, Frank Stapleton, Jimmy Conway from Fulham and David Langan from Derby County. What a line-up! I togged out again with the Past XI. The previous year the local newspapers would not take any story before the match was played. But this time it was a little different. There were no less than three different write-ups before the match. I suppose that with so many big names mentioned they felt that it was worth taking a chance. Some details of the players involved are as follows: four full Irish internationals, David O'Leary and Frank Stapleton, both of Arsenal, Jimmy Conway (Fulham) and Dave Langan (Derby County), Graham Rix (Arsenal) – English under-age international soon to become a full international – and Martin Welsh under-eighteen international. Such a galaxy of stars never appeared in a junior match around there before. But there is a bit more: David O'Leary's father, Christy, took the referee's whistle for this match and the famous league of Ireland player, Bunny Fullam, ex-Drumcondra, also took part in the match.

There was also another competition – to find out the underage penalty king for 1977. The finalists were John Casey, Pat Griffin, Martin Power, Brendan Power, Richard Casey and Colin Purcell. The trophies for this competition were sponsored by my father, Ben. The past team cruised to a 4–1 win. Frank Stapleton, who scored so many goals for Arsenal and Ireland, left his mark on Alaska Park with two goals. David O'Leary scored one goal and a former colleague of mine in the 1950s, Sonny Power, scored the other. After the game there was a celebratory dance in the nearby CSM ballroom in Clonea which all the guests attended and at which they were besieged by autograph hunters. The souvenir trophies for both sides were sponsored by the local banks and presented by the club chairman P. Cahill. Before he left the village, Jimmy Conway presented the club with one of his international jerseys.

I had decided that the 1978 exhibition in Kilmac would be the final one. Those three functions, in my opinion, would be an adequate way of celebrating the twenty-fifth year of the club's existence – its silver anniversary. I had given some thought about what should be done for this last one and decided that I would bring all Irish international players for this. I had started planning for it in the early part of the 1976–7 season. My friend, Jimmy Conway, was not available. He had been transferred from Manchester City to Portland Timbers in Oregon, USA. When I approached the two Arsenal players who had been in the 1977 match, David O'Leary and Frank Stapleton, they agreed to travel. There were two other Irish international players at Arsenal: Liam Brady, who had been an international star for a number of years, and John Devine, at this stage an under-21 international, soon to become a full cap. I approached both of them and found out that they would be delighted to attend. The only other player that I approached, was Dave Langan of Derby County. He was one of the 1977 players. He had received a further honour – he had just been elected player of the year at Derby County for 1977 and he said he would be delighted to go back to Kilmac!

A problem arose. Liam Brady was injured in the English FA cup final and was forced to come off. He also had to miss Ireland's international match in Denmark. But he confirmed that he would be in attendance and willing to sign for autograph hunters. Mr Paddy Daly, the well-known Irish international and League of Ireland referee, came from Dublin to take charge. There was as couple of other interesting occurrences. Kilmacthomas has an excellent GAA complex and when they heard of all the stars who would be in attendance they magnanimously made their dressing rooms available. That was very much appreciated. A far cry from when the GAA club of the time (1949) ejected a thirteen-year-old boy (me) from their coach because he had seen a soccer match in Waterford.

I was happy when a knock on the door at Tramore (where we stayed) brought Liam Brady, who had interrupted his holiday in Kerry to be with us. And more, when we got to Kilmacthomas, he said that he would appear as guest goalkeeper in the past team. The game took place before the biggest attendance ever at the local Alaska Park. Liam Brady also made the Beatty Trophy presentations to the three school boys, Pat Halloran, Brendan Power and Colin Purcell for the under–fourteen penalty awards. After all that the match was won easily by the Past team. All the stars participated. It was an excellent exhibition, really appreciated by the large attendance. To round off this big attraction a dance was held at O'Shea's Hotel, Tramore, which all the guests attended. After dinner tremendous celebrations went on to the early hours. All the players from both sides were presented by the club with appropriate mementoes, sponsored by local businesses. This whole episode, now concluded, will be something remembered forever in Kilmacthomas.

The Kilmac soccer story really started on the 27 March 1949. On a fine Sunday I went out after my lunch for a walk around the 'small ring'. A car pulled up in front of me. Percy Kirwan was in the car. He called me over and said 'Tony, would you like to come into Kilcohan Park with me to see Waterford play Drumcondra?' As I used to call into his shop every week to discuss Waterford's match on the previous Sunday – he used to go regularly to the matches – I thought, 'What a good idea.' I went with him and we saw what was for me a very interesting match. Waterford lost 3–2. When I got home and told my parents, there cannot have been any problems, or, if there were, I cannot remember them. Anyway the following week I carried on my training with the local minor hurling team. Somebody had heard about my trip to Kilcohan Park and warned me that I would be reported under the dreaded Rule 27. That was the infamous rule that banned GAA members from watching or playing 'foreign games' like soccer, rugby or hockey. But I could not believe that anybody would report me.

We had trained hard. I was the youngest player in the hurling squad. Nobody had mentioned foreign games after that. When the big day dawned the excitement was something special. We were to be at the post office at 12 o'clock to pick up a coach to Dungarvan to travel to the match we were excitedly looking forward to. So far as I know, this was the very first time that Kilmac Hurling Club had ever entered a team in the Waterford Minor Hurling Championship. As the players entered the bus we had to pass two of the officials on their way to the seats. We all had our hurleys with socks and boots tied round them. When my turn came I went up the steps and reached the officials. One put his hand up, stopped me and said, 'You are not coming. You attended a soccer match in Waterford and under Rule 27 you are banned. Leave the bus.' I was thirteen years old. On my way home I think the tears started. The minors were hammered in their match.

Two or three months later I thought 'Would it be possible to form a local soccer team?' I started asking around and found a few lads interested in having a go.

By August I had ten ex-Gaelic footballers interested. By the end of the year I had fourteen lads who were keen. Then I got a few lads together as a committee. We decided we would need a set of jerseys. But a problem: we had no money. I agreed to approach Mr Kirwan. He was delighted to hear of our plans. When we told him about the jerseys, he volunteered to put up the cash required as a loan which could be repaid over a few years. We looked for red-and-white jerseys. By mistake we got maroon-and-white. The price was £12/7s/6d (£12.87.5), which Mr Kirwan paid.

We were on our way. The training was, we thought, going well. A few months had gone by. We were now in mid-1950. So I tried to arrange some matches. It was not easy. Eventually our first match was arranged some time in September 1950, for the first Sunday in November 1950, away to Dawn Rovers of Kilmeaden. But, before that, we formally convened the club at a meeting in the courthouse on 16 September 1950.

For our first match we all excitedly took the Waterford bus on Sunday 5 November. Even my father came with us. The Dawn Rovers ground was called Spa Park. For us it was very exciting. Nobody had a camera that day, so no photo was taken. Dawn Rovers looked like professionals to us in our new maroon-and-white shirts and red-and-white socks. Of course we were outclassed. I have the score down as us losing 5–1. It could have been more. It was Billy Burke who scored our first-ever goal.

Our next game was on 27 January 1951, at Scrahan Park, also against Dawn Rovers. What a difference! The result was 4–4. The season went on we got more used to the game. We played ten matches altogether – nine friendlies, and our first-ever championship match in the Infirmary Cup at home to St Patrick's Athletic. It was understood that Percy Kirwan would accept the role of president. We had the following working and selection committee members: R. Fleming, P. Gallagher, B. Beatty, G. Flynn, E. Russell, J. McCarthy. At a slightly later stage, H. Hamilton joined the committee. A minor team was formed and elected to the league in 1952–3.

The following is a sample of the tributes paid to Percy Kirwan (1881–1969), without whom the club would not have existed. One journalist had this to say:

> If one were to single out a great sportsman and lovable Irishman of Co. Waterford and to know Percy Kirwan of Kilmacthomas, intimately, one's selection would be very easy indeed. He is possessed of all those grand traits of character for which the Irish race is respected throughout the world, for he is the embodiment of the word sportsman and gentleman. There is no greater enthusiast for any manly form of sport, be it athletics, horse racing, boxing, soccer, Gaelic or rugby. Furthermore, he is always ready to give all possible assistance to any club requiring it, but with his characteristic unobstrusiveness does so from behind the scenes and where it is most needed.

For me to meet someone of the calibre of Mr Kirwan just once in a lifetime is a privilege. I had that privilege. His achievement in athletics – he was winner of the British AAA long jump championship in three successive years, 1910, 1911 and 1912 – puts him into the realms of world superstars. He also played Gaelic football for Waterford. I have already indicated what his friendship meant to me – a Currabaha schoolboy in the mid- and late-1940s. I have told the story of how Mr Percy Kirwan became father, patron and creator of Kilmacthomas soccer club. On walks with him around the 'Big Ring' we talked a lot about the development of the club and he advised on many occasions of the type of training we should do. I can never properly express my appreciation of such a man.

When my father retired from the post office in 1968, he came frequently to London on holidays. Then in 1977 he came to live permanently with my sister Patsy and her husband Denis in Whetstone, North London. During that time his grandchildren in London got to know him better. The first time I took Paul and Ian to meet him in London (they had only met him briefly on our visits to Ireland) they got on great. The boys spent some time with him and they chatted about everything: school, sports, hobbies. On our way home it was interesting to hear their comments. In particular I can recall Paul saying, 'I enjoyed talking to Grandad, he's really nice,' and Ian agreed with him.

He settled down very well at my sister's and had a daily routine. After breakfast he walked to the shops to buy the paper, came home, picked out his horses and went to the bookmakers to place his bets. After lunch he watched the races on television. He loved to meet people and got to know a lot of new people through myself, Patsy and Denis. He was content with his new life. After 1977 he went back to Ireland only once on holidays. Early in 1979 he got ill and was not recovering. Time went on; his health got worse. Christmas 1979 arrived and it was obvious that he was deteriorating. Early in 1980 we had to face the reality that his illness was terminal. He bravely carried on as long as he could. It was very upsetting to see our dad, who had been so fit and active all his life, confined to his bed. I used to call to see him every morning on my way to work and, despite his condition, he still picked his horses every day. Even on his last morning, he had his bet ready for me. In retrospect, I think that at that stage he was doing it more for me than for himself. He died peacefully on 23 May 1980.

We had a funeral Mass for him at St Mary Magdalen's church in Whetstone and we then accompanied his remains to Ireland where he was laid to rest beside my mother in All Saint's cemetery, Newtown, County Waterford. May he rest in peace.

A final story about my county of Waterford in south-east Ireland. The county allegedly has an unusual phenomenon in addition to as the tourist attractions of the Comeragh mountains. The Mahon River goes through my native village of Kilmacthomas on its journey to the sea at Bonmahon. Its journey starts at the attractive Mahon Falls in the Comeragh Mountains. I had heard an interesting story of a strange thing that happens on the road down to the Mahon Falls. The story suggested that cars roll backwards uphill on their own without any help from the driver. There are many different theories as to why this happens; there was talk of digging up the road to find out if there are any magnetic reasons. As yet no reason has ever been found. When I go home to Waterford on holidays I stay in Lemybrien, with my sister Eileen and her family. From there roads lead up to Mahon Falls in the Comeraghs. Before he died on 15 November 2000 my uncle, Tommy Power, who lived in Kilmacthomas, used to arange to take me for a trip to various parts of the county and to many other places of interest. One of the most interesting things about those trips was that I never knew in advance where we would end up.

On one of these trips in June 1998 this is what happened: he phoned me at my sister's house and arranged for us to meet. He picked me up and away we went. It soon became clear that we were heading for the Comeragh mountains. When I asked him during the journey (which was a strange one to me) about our destination, his response was, 'Wait and see.' We passed a sign which indicated that we were on the way to the Mahon Falls. Of course, like most people from Waterford, I had heard of the 'backwards' road, but also, like most people from the area, I took the story for granted and never bothered to pursue it. When I asked my uncle about it he said that we were now on the 'magic' road and told me to watch out for a hawthorn bush. We found the bush and then my uncle stopped the car. Believe it or not the car then started to travel backwards up the hill with no power. What more can I say!

9

THE IRISH CENTRE

I helped many charities that needed help when I was in a position to do the necessary. My reason for taking on the Irish Centre was a bit different. My firm, Beatty & Company, was the centre's auditors so I was all too aware of their financial problems. When the priest in charge, Fr Claude Malone, heard of my efforts for other charities, he asked me if I would attempt to do something similar for the centre. They had very heavy debts and he admitted to me that the tide was out as far as it could go. Obviously, because of my background and my deep-rooted interest in the welfare of the Irish community, he saw me as the ideal candidate to remedy the situation and I agreed to take a look at their problem. That problem was so bad that when I talked to my colleagues their advice was: 'Leave it alone.' The centre was not only broke, it was in debt to the tune of about £1 million to builders, the bank and other creditors. In financial terms, it was suffering from a terminal illness.

After studying the situation, I decided to ignore other professional advice. The saving of the Irish Centre, which had its site in Camden Town, represented a challenge – probably the biggest professional challenge of my life – and I agreed to give it a go, strictly on my terms. I told Fr Malone that if he wanted to get my help it would have to be done my way, without any outside interference whatsoever. I told him that I would not answer to any committee but would provide regular progress reports to the priests-in-charge regularly. 'Just do the things you were ordained to do,' I told him, 'and leave the rest to me.' I knew that if he agreed to these conditions, there was a fair chance I would be able to solve the centre's problems within a few years.

Negotiations with creditors were tough but they were mostly fair in their attitude. After all, if the centre was declared bankrupt and fell into the hands of the receiver, they would receive only a small fraction of their outstanding debts. They accepted that my way was the best long-term solution and this considerably eased the pressure. Firstly I had to wheel and deal to arrange a long-term loan at the best possible rate to extricate the centre from the mire and then I set about pulling in some desperately needed finance from charity events and sponsorship by London-based Irish business houses. When I started to get results through my many negotiations with creditors and others the priests involved, Fr Malone and Fr Butler, were, of course, delighted, although the centre's committees were not happy; but they knew my conditions. Much of the charity calendar embraced golf days which, in turn, attracted additional sponsorship. I organised, through the Waterford Association Golf Society (later the Waterford Golfing Society), five big golf days which highlighted the problems and difficulties encountered by the Irish Centre. Those days also showed the extent of the support available for such a project if somebody makes the effort to seek such support. It is not easy to do and only by getting involved will one realise what it entails.

I had no idea of what to expect but hard work does create its own rewards. Just as on the first ever golf day which I organised for the Benburb Base, another Irish charity, I felt very nervous about this one. I was really laying it on the line for everybody. The people approached to be sponsors and the players were delighted to be given the opportunity to help. The number of golfers who took part was 184 and the sponsors totalled twenty-five. A few Irish sporting celebrities took part, and the authenticity of the day was highlighted by the presence at the event of the Irish Ambassador, Dr Eamonn Kennedy, who made the trophy presentations to the day's golf competition winners. In my message on the day's brochure I thanked the two priests involved, Fr C. Malone and Fr J. Butler, for their work on behalf of the Irish community. I also thanked our Ambassador to the Court of St James for his attendance and help. So, all in all, it was a good start. In their message the priests highlighted the problem of the massive debt and thanked everybody involved for their support. The kind words said about me were appreciated. They also thanked the famous sports stars whom I was able to get to attend. I refer to the four Irish international football stars, David O'Leary and John Devine from Arsenal, Gerry Ryan from Brighton and Hove Albion, plus Tony Grealish. Although those lads had very busy schedules they took time to attend, play golf, sign autographs and help in any way they could. With support like this, how could one go wrong!

After this event, something special happened. The major area of the Centre, MacNamara Hall, badly needed an up-market entrance lobby. Well, £10,000 of this day's proceeds was used to build it and, as such, was a worthwhile way of proving that the local Irish community will support their own. This was also a way of boosting my own confidence. Fr Malone made his feelings clear in the 1982 brochure:

> When I took on the directorship of the Irish Centre last November the massive debt of the Centre honestly frightened me and I really felt like the man looking down the deep dark tunnel – all I would see was darkness and gloom and I felt quite powerless to bring in a ray of light.

This ray of light that now acts as my inspiration and gives my heart a lift comes from the rallying around of a bunch of friends of the Irish Centre called the Waterford Association in London. Through their efforts this sponsored golf-day promises to be a great success. I am sure that the Waterford Association would want me to put the record straight by pointing out and acknowledging the man who gave birth to the idea and who put so much into the organisation of this event. I refer to Mr Tony Beatty.

The work for the centre continued. The second annual golf day took place on 23 March 1983. One of the highlights was the presence on the course and afterwards in cabaret of the brilliant comedian Niall Toibin, who insisted in paying all his own expenses. I managed with the ever-present help of such stalwarts as John (RIP) and Cathy Dee and Garry Hill and many other generous supporters and sponsors to organise more 'days' on 4 April 1984, 24 April 1985 and 23 April 1986. The effect was to save the centre and to put its financial future on a sounder basis. So many friends, bishops, ambassadors, businessmen, conscious of the worth of the centre's work and of its care of newer waves of Irish immigrants, rallied to the centre's assistance.

A telephone call in midsummer 1988 from Fr Bobby Gilmore, head of the Irish chaplaincy in Britain, was the first inkling that there was something special on the horizon. I had first met him during my close association with the Irish Centre. He first advised me not to get too excited and then he broke the news that my name had been included among the nominations for a special papal award. He said these are given very sparingly to individuals worldwide for certain types of charitable and other good works. I was nominated, he informed me, for two reasons: for having the idea which became the *Irish Post*, which was now accepted as having played a major role in uniting the Irish community in Britain, for my work in helping to save the Irish Centre from financial ruin and for other charitable works. He would be in touch again, he told me, when a decision had been made.

I was walking on air for the next few days. To be nominated for such an accolade simply for achieving two things which had brought me tremendous personal satisfaction seemed mildly incongruous but I would be lying if I suggested that I was anything less than extremely proud that my achievements had been recognised. Not that I expected to receive an award: far from it. It was praise indeed to have been nominated. I saw it as a slight deviation from that popular maxim which seems to epitomise life: 'Many are called but few are chosen.' But a papal award was different. More a case of 'Few are called and even fewer are chosen.'

When Father Gilmore telephoned a few weeks later to tell me that I had been selected as one of only two UK recipients of the award, my heart (but I hope not my head) swelled with pride. It was a rare moment when both mind and body unite to share an experience of the highest elation. It seemed unbelievable and it fleetingly crossed my mind that 'somebody up there' was perhaps trying in some way to atone for the cruel strokes of fate which had robbed me of my son and my sister, and had left me crippled. (I will never recover from the death of my elder son, who died so tragically in a car accident on 15 May 1985 at the age of just twenty-one.)

I learned that I was to receive the gold Benemerenti medal with a personalised scroll signed by no lesser authority than His Holiness Pope John-Paul II. It occurred to me that I had been aware of the pope's existence all my life. Now, perhaps for a fleeting second as he signed my scroll, the pope had been aware of the existence of Bernard Anthony Beatty, a boy from Kimacthomas who had made it in London. The presentation

Mass was held on Saturday 15 October 1988 at the church of Our Lady and St George's, and it is a memory I shall cherish to the end of my days. The church was packed with friends and family, many of whom had journeyed from Ireland specially for the occasion. They mingled with the normal Mass attendance,

The presentation was made, appropriately, by Fr Gilmore, this time acting as the pope's messenger as well as attending in his official capacity as head of the Irish chaplaincy. When he concluded his address, during which he said some embarrassingly nice things about me, the congregation broke into spontaneous applause. I had never heard people clap in church before, and I found it quite unnerving. Then, as I looked around the congregation it occurred to me that the last time we had all been together in the same church was the day of Paul's funeral Mass. I nodded my gratitude with tears in my eyes and a lump in my throat, and I could think only of Paul.

It strikes me that this might be an appropriate place to insert a personal word from Fr Jim Butler OMI, who was the Irish Centre chaplain:

> My introduction to the author of this book (Tony Beatty) was a very gradual affair. After all he was living a long way from the centre of London and I resided at the Irish Centre in Camden in central London.
>
> His visits to the Irish Centre were not all that frequent and they were strictly businesslike. There was a meeting to be attended to – the meeting was over – time to go home. I might have met him – again I might not have met him.
>
> In time I became aware of the existence of an Irish Centre Golfing Society. Being a golfer I very quickly became a member, only to find that it was

headed by Tony Beatty.

Golf became a catalyst – soon I began to know the man Tony Beatty and his intense interest in all things Irish in London.

The Irish Centre was set up in the 1950s to cater for all those thousands of young Irish people coming to London to look for work. By degrees social workers were employed to afford professional advice. Some boys received accommodation at the Irish Centre itself in Camden and some girls received accommodation in a small girls' hostel in Highgate.

Funds to service these hostels came mainly from functions held at the Irish Centre itself, e.g. dinner dances, dances, bacon-and-cabbage functions and various social events and fundraising activities.

As more adequate accommodation became mandatory for both boys and girls so too did more adequate facilities for fundraising events. This involved the building of a new functions hall, new kitchens and entrance facilities. The price was horrendous.

Soon these new facilities became functional and more frequent and larger functions became the order of the day. Excellent! But the proceeds in no way measured up to the demands of repayments and interest.

This is where the crisis emerged. Despite the greatest endeavours of management and staff at the Irish Centre in no way could they meet their commitments.

This is where Tony Beatty came in. He saw what was happening. He knew what had to be done and he decided to give it his everything. He first of all put proper bookkeeping procedures in place. This involved keeping his staff on the premises until these procedures were set up and explained to Irish Centre personnel.

The debt was in the region of £1.1 million – the demands were horrendous and the resources were almost non-existent.

But by his professional expertise and financial ingenuity he gradually got to grips with the problem, faced all the obstacles in his path and, little by little and major achievement by major achievement, he finally reached the point where all the debt could be cleared, all the interest paid and the Irish Centre once again placed on a healthy financial footing. For this the Irish Centre owes him its eternal gratitude.

To think that all this was achieved without the slightest regard for remuneration must be the most wonderful tribute to the generosity of the man who had given his all to salvage a sinking Irish Centre. No doubt he was inspired to go all-out by his lifelong interest in the Irish people in London, his admiration for the emigrants from Ireland who were desperately striving to better themselves, his sincere sympathy for those who found it hard to achieve their ambitions and his very personal commitment to support all things Irish in whatever way he could.

Tony Beatty never got a payment for any of his work in freeing the Irish Centre from its crippling debt. All his services were at all times entirely free.

Indeed his Charity Golf Days raised over £60,000, not including his own personal contributions. Not only did he give his professional services entirely free but he went out of his way and inconvenienced himself in an unlimited degree in involving himself in these fundraising activities.

It really is quite impossible to summarise Tony Beatty's contribution to the Irish Centre in London. To be an onlooker at all this achievement and to witness the constant devotion to the job in hand – to rid the Irish Centre of its crippling debt – was a privilege rarely afforded to people. I was that lucky onlooker and that wondering witness.

On a personal level it was a great privilege to have known Tony Beatty and to be in some way privy to what was at stake and what was involved. How he applied his entrepreneurial insights along with his professional expertise to the monumental task of clearing a £1.1 million debt in such a short space of time leaves one spellbound and indeed in a state of intense admiration.

I would like to pay tribute to Tony Beatty and to all his achievements. His solving of the Irish Centre debt would only be one of his distinguished achievements but it is the one I know most about and I was there during the crisis.

On behalf of all the Oblates who served at the Irish Centre, on behalf of all the administrative committees, on behalf of all the staff, social workers and Centre staff, on behalf of all the people who were helped at the Irish Centre in Camden in London, on behalf of all those who, through the Irish Centre, scaled the heights in business, politics, the services and indeed the Church itself – a big 'Thank you, Tony.'

I recommend the book and hope that you too will be inspired not only to scale the heights in business yourself but that you will come to the rescue of those who find the climbing tough.

Fr Jim Butler OMI
(Chaplain to the Irish Centre 1977–83)

IRELAND ALWAYS

When I went to see Ireland play away to England in Wembley on 8 May 1957 it was just because the match was on and I was able to go. When I went back to Ireland a couple of weeks later as I hoped for good, I only dreamed about ever seeing them play again and as for travelling with them... That all changed when the *Irish Post* started up and I met the Fulham and Ireland international player, Jimmy Conway.

From my first trip in May 1975 I always travelled with the officials and the players and, as a result, I got to know many of the members of the teams. If on that day in Wembley in 1957 I was told this I would probably have said something like: 'Pull the other one.' But I am very happy to be able to say, 'It is all true.'

When I started to read the sports pages of the daily and weekend newspapers in some detail, probably some time in 1946, I realised that Ireland had two international soccer teams, one representing 'Eire,' the Twenty-Six-County team, later to become the Republic of Ireland Football Association of Ireland (FAI) and the other representing Northern Ireland, the Irish Football Association (IFA). That was the situation when I got to hear of two great players, Peter Doherty (Derby County and Northern Ireland) and Johnny (Jackie) Carey (Manchester United and 'Eire'). At this time the FAI chose their team from players born in the twenty-six counties only but Northern Ireland could choose a team from players born in any of the counties of Ireland, north or south. That position changed in 1950 and since then each side can choose only players born in their own part of the country.

When I had absorbed all the above information I realised that obviously the team I would support was the one representing the Republic of Ireland. Until I emigrated in July 1955 I read everything I could find that had to do with international football where Ireland was involved. I suppose I thought that something not irrelevant might happen when I was in England, living in St Albans. However, I got so involved in playing soccer myself and involved in other pastimes that, apart from keeping an eye on results as the papers reported them, my interest in international matches was no longer a priority. My time for going home permanently (as I thought) after two years abroad was coming closer. One of my football friends from the Herts county league team I played with, Ballito Sports, told me about the forthcoming World Cup match at Wembley Stadium between England and the Republic of Ireland. Two of my football friends decided to come with me.

My friends and I really looked forward to the big match in Wembley. On the train trip to London my friends emphasised that England would win by a 'few' goals. Of course I took my country's side and said we would win. It was a World Cup match and, in those years, goal difference did not count. Just as well because we were absolutely hammered, by five goals to one. It was embarrassing, and my return trip to St Albans was one time when I wished I were not an Irish fan. Some days later the return fixture was played in Dublin. I knew that a one-goal win in that match would be enough for us. I did not go to Dublin but listened in to the radio commentary with my English friends. Before the match they confidently said that England would 'slaughter' us. What could I say apart from the comment that we were kidding last week. I thought after the Wembley match that we had no chance but football is a funny game. Ireland played out of their skins in Dublin. On the radio commentary, from the absolute start, Ireland seemed to be as much on top as England were in the first match. When Ireland took the lead and looked like scoring more my friends got very quiet. The ninety minutes ended and we were still one-nil up. Revenge is sweet, I thought. Then, in the second minute of injury time, England scored the equaliser, totally against the run of play. That draw was enough to put England through and Ireland out of the World Cup. About eighteen years elapsed before I saw Ireland play away again, in Kiev, for the match against Russia.

From the mid-1960s onwards I seldom missed a home international match – all played in Dublin. I had built up many contacts and it had been suggested on a few occasions that I should consider travelling abroad with the people who went with the team – as a member of the official party. Time went on and the next away match took place on 18 May 1975 against Russia in Kiev, in the European championship. Breda came with me and we had a lovely trip. There was a couple of interesting events on this trip.

As I related earlier, on the Sunday I served my first and last Mass and we managed to fulfilled our religious obligations. A coach tour had been arranged for us to view the countryside in the vicinity of Kiev. This was most enjoyable. Passing along and watching the locals working in the fields was fascinating. It was then time to go to the stadium for the match.

After the Russian match we flew to Switzerland to meet the home side, also in the European championships, in Berne. This was a game Ireland expected to win. In the couple of days before the match we went through the shops and bought some interesting souvenirs to bring back to the family and on the night before the match all our official party were taken to the Irish embassy in Geneva. It was a memorable experience. The match was played on 21 May 1975. Although our team had an excellent match they just could not score. In one of their rare attacks Switzerland scored, held on to their lead and the game ended Switzerland 1: Ireland nil.

The next away match I attended was against almost a home fixture, for me and for many other supporters. It was against England at Wembley stadium on 8 September 1976. Ireland played really well and the result was a 1–1 draw. This time the Irish team were, in the opinion of many onlookers, unlucky not to win. But, at least, it was not another 'away' defeat. We live in hope!

When I heard of the next away match, in Paris against France on 17 November 1976, I knew that this was one that I could not beear to miss. The excitement in the build-up to the match was immense and I was really looking forward to this meeting between two well-matched sides. When it finally started, the first half-hour was very even and we hoped that we could get a good result. But in the second half the home side seemed to be on a different wavelength and they finally won by two goals to nil. We thought that a draw would have been a fairer result. But, again, we were the 'unlucky' losers. It must surely get better soon.

My next trip was to Sofia to see the match, Bulgaria v Ireland, on 1 June 1977. This was a very interesting tour. From the time we arrived in Sofia I decided to find out as much as I could about the place. I went into the shops to get some souvenirs and presents. I found out that there was a coach tour for the people on the tour on the day before the match, organised by the hotel. We toured the countryside around Sofia and it was all strange to me. It gave a clear indication about how the people lived and made their livelihoods. It was a very enjoyable trip and the tour guide gave full details of the places we passed through and pointed out anything of interest that we should see. She was very precise in her explanations. We really enjoyed her talk until, on our way back to the hotel, when she used some time to 'explain' about how good it was to live in a country like Bulgaria rather than in the western world!

It was time to look forward to the match. In retrospect I must say that of all the away matches I attended, this was by far the most unlucky result for the Irish that I saw. Ireland were very good and it seemed that it was only a matter of time until they scored. But football, as I may have remarked before, is a funny game. Ireland scored what we thought was a good goal. The referee did not agree with us and disallowed it. In the end, against all the odds, Bulgaria won by two goals to one. On the records, it will be shown as just another away defeat.

In 1978 I went on a tour which included two countries I had never visited before. The venues were in Scandinavia and the first match was a friendly against Norway in the capital, Oslo. There were coach tours available and as usual I took one which gave an excellent indication of what the countryside near Oslo was like. We also travelled to the footballers' training ground to watch them go through their training exercises. Kick-off time came and I remember thinking at the time that it was probably one of the most boring matches that I had ever seen. This result, on 21 May 1978, was a stupefying nil-nil draw. On reflection, neither side deserved to win. From a football point of view I was very pleased to leave Norway and make for Denmark.

From the time we arrived in Copenhagen I noted that the whole football atmosphere was different. At that time, the Danish team were just beginning to develop as one of Europe's best. The match against Denmark was played in Copenhagen on 24 May 1978. After the Oslo result I, like many of the travelling supporters, thought that we had no chance. Before the match I, as chairman of the *Irish Post*, had a very pleasant duty to carry out. It was on this trip that I presented the paper's sports star award to Liverpool's Steve Heighway, who had been overseas with his team on the day the awards were presented in London. I arranged with a local newspaper to send a photographer along and the photo was published shortly after in the *Irish Post*.

Now, back to the football. To show just how unpredictable the game is, Ireland played like world champions and, in fact, should have won. It was a wonderful contest: – in fact with less than ten minutes to go, the score was Denmark 1 : Ireland 3. But a thrilling finish by the home side allowed them to score two goals (one a penalty) in about eight minutes and the final whistle came with the score three goals each. The excitement of this great match is something I will never forget. In fact, considering every international match I ever saw, I would have to say that this one was undoubtedly the best.

My support of my team continued as the years went by. In 1979 I was in Swansea to watch a disappointing match against Wales in which our Celtic kin beat us 2–1. I was back in Wembley on 6 February 1980 to see a lacklustre Ireland being beaten 2–0 by a undistinguished English side. I thought to myself it might change, sometime. Well, dreams cost nothing. That October the much-travelled Beatty was back in Paris to see his team deservedly beaten 2–0 by la belle France.

In 1981 I made two trips, the first one to Brussels for a match against Belgium. The match was organised for the evening of 25 March 1981. As usual we went there on the Sunday, a couple of days in advance, and, again, I used that time to go on a coach tour. Brussels is a beautiful city and is so small compared to London. Then going to watch the players going through their training schedules was enjoyable. In due course it was time to go to the stadium for this World Cup match. We, Ireland, needed a good result to have a chance of getting to the finals. As it carried on Ireland looked by far the better side. But the usual problem: no goals. Then, a few minutes before half-time, our striker, Frank Stapleton, broke through and scored what we considered to be an excellent goal. We were celebrating – but wait: the referee blew his whistle and disallowed our goal. Why? Nobody seemed to know. Even to this day that goal that wasn't a goal is discussed at length.

That was bad, but worse was to come. The second half was a bit more open than the first. The ninety minutes seemed to be up and the score was still nil-nil. A draw was all that we needed. We were happy. But then Belgium got a free kick. The ball floated into the Irish penalty area. Our goalkeeper, Seamus McDonagh, went towards the ball but, before he got there, he clashed with a forward and appeared to have been fouled. A Belgium forward reached the cross and headed it into the net. But we weren't worried as we felt sure that we would have a free kick. But the referee whistled and instead of giving a free out, he allowed the goal. Then the whistle blew again. Full time and another 'unlucky' defeat by one goal to nil.

That September I was in Rotterdam to see Ireland take on a team that was at the time one of Europe's best sides – Holland. I found it to be a very interesting country and when I took the opportunity to go on a tour from the hotel, I discovered it to be a very historic place. After that tour there was the usual period of viewing the team in training and discussing its against the home side. The local papers gave us no chance but again to prove the uncertainty of the game, we saw an excellent match. The result was a 2–2 draw between two very well-balanced teams. Both sides could say with confidence that they deserved to win. So on reflection, a draw was a very fair result.

When I travelled again, just over a year later, coincidentally it was to Rotterdam again. The match against Holland was on 22 September 1982. It was again closely contested by two good sides but this time Holland shaded it to win by two goals to one in an excellent match. On this trip I was accompanied by my good friend, Terry McIntyre, and during our visit we went on a trip to The Hague to visit the Irish Embassy.

The next away match was in Malta, the holiday island. This was very special. I contacted my brother John in Ireland and invited him to join me on this trip. He was delighted to come and, with the squad, we flew to Valetta on Sunday afternoon, 28 March 1983, for the match scheduled to be played on 30 March. It was a fascinating trip. On the Monday we went on two different coach tours of the island and enjoyed viewing the beautiful scenery. The food in the hotel was great, certainly not appropriate for somebody watching their weight. As usual, engaging with the players involved was a build-up to the match on Tuesday night. It was great going to the training ground and watching the men preparing. This time there was an unusual difference in the team hotel. For the first time on my many trips abroad, Ireland were the favourites.

The match started. From the beginning Ireland were well on top, but with the usual 'away' problem, they just could not score. No score at half-time. In the second half, with no score still towards the end, it was clear that frustration was beginning to take effect. Ninety minutes came and, for a team to be so much on top and still not have scored was, to put it mildly, very annoying. But then, in the second minute of injury time, Frank Stapleton scored to give us a 1–0 victory. This was the first away victory I had witnessed up to this point.

Although I did not know it at the time, the trip to Japan was my last tour with the Irish squad, due to the state of my illness, which was unfortunately developing quite quickly. Soon there was no way that I would be able to travel with the team again. But, therein lies a story. My trip to Japan with the Irish international team, when I was accompanied by Breda, was by far the best one. The competition was the Japan Cup 1984. The flight to Tokyo lasted about fifteen hours, with a refuelling stop in Anchorage, Alaska. We finally got to our base and from the beginning we saw how different it was to the western world. Now that I think about it, those next couple of weeks made one of the most enjoyable holidays that Breda and I ever had.

The first two matches, against Japan University on 27 May, and the famous FC International (Brazil) on the 1 June, were both played in Tokyo and ended as scoreless draws. But, because of the way other matches ended, Ireland was in the semi-final, which was played in Sapporo against China on the 3 June. Ireland won this match by one goal to nil. When that match was played we were on holiday, within the holiday, in a place called Kyoto. Whilst there we went on two coach tours and found it a strange and fascinating place.

Ireland was in an international soccer final for the first time ever. The opponents were FC International (Brazil) for the second time in the tournament. It was a most exciting match at Tokyo's Olympic stadium. Despite having taken the lead, Ireland lost by two goals to one. At least history was made for Ireland when they reached the final. We returned home on the 6 June. On a personal point, I have to state that this was a wonderful way to end my travelling with the Irish team. Of course, at that stage, I thought that I could go on and on. After that trip, my mobility deteriorated and I can now only thank God that I was able to attend so many international matches in so many different countries. Japan was like saving the best wine till last.

In the mid-1980s I thought, in the middle of a period of MS remission, that I would like to go along to watch a match with a couple of friends who were involved with a non-league club. The club was Haringey Borough FC, which at that time played in the Vauxhall Opel league. I enjoyed what I saw. No doubt part of the reason for this was the fact that when I played football Haringey Borough were known as Wood Green Town. I played against them on two occasions. But now, towards the end of the 1985-6 season, my friends asked if I would be interested in becoming a member of the club committee. I told them that I would be delighted to get involved but, due to my illness, this could be short-term. Yet because of my interest in the game they insisted that they wanted me. I really enjoyed my involvement with the team. During the pre-season training for 1986–7 the committee decided on a trip to Ireland for a game against the League of Ireland club, Bray Wanderers. It was a most enjoyable trip and certainly enhanced team spirit.

The 1986–7 season started and the club had an excellent record, finishing third out of twenty-two teams and missing promotion by just a couple of points. Towards the close of season I was asked at a committee meeting if I could use my Irish connections to arrange a 1987–8 pre-season tour of the south east of Ireland. I arranged three matches against Waterford at Kilcohan Park, against EMFA (now Kilkenny City) at Buckley Park and my home town, Kilmacthomas, at Alaska Park, Kilmacthomas. In Waterford I arranged a visit to Waterford Crystal, which went down very well with the visitors, as did an official welcome to Waterford by the Lord Mayor of Waterford. In the three matches Haringey lost to Waterford, drew with Kilkenny and beat Kilmacthomas. There was a very interesting conclusion to this. My son Ian, who was on holiday from university, travelled with us. He was chosen by the manager to play against Kilmacthomas and appointed captain for the day. It was a proud moment for me to see him play on my old home ground against the team of which I was a founder member.

The 1987–8 season got under way but, unfortunately, in early October, I suffered an MS relapse and felt I couldn't carry on taking an active role in the club. After the club had fulfilled five league matches, I had to resign as a committee member. It was quite a bad relapse and my mobility was gradually getting worse. So, sadly, my involvement with Haringey Borough Football Club ended in October 1987.

After a few months out of football, and during a further remission stage of my disease, I was approached by one of the directors of Hendon football club with a view to my joining them. I felt quite flattered and told them so. I also explained that about my MS and that I could get a relapse without warning but I would keep going as long as I could. I explained that I would have to step down if and when I got a relapse. They emphasised that they wanted me to join despite my health problem. They also indicated that if I joined I would be proposed as chairman at their next AGM in late May 1988. Knowing their reputation as a very respected senior non-league club, I agreed to join. Over the next few months I had some of the most interesting experiences that I every had in football and I propose to share some of them with you.

First of all, in late May I was elected chairman. Then I had an experience that can never be repeated. Before I was elected, the club had reached the final of the Middlesex Senior Charity Cup, and it was mentioned that the final would be played at Wembley Stadium. Every football person wants to get to Wembley in some official capacity. Well we were there and the path to the final was as follows: bye in the preliminary round, beat Haringey Borough 3–0 in the first round, beat Hayes 1–0 in the second round, beat Finchley 2–0 in the semi-final, then in the final at the famous stadium, beat another Vauxhall Opel league team Wembley by 2–0. The celebrations then took over for a while. Then something fascinating was pointed out to me. This final was my first ever match as chairman of Hendon Football Club. Apparently, nobody had ever had his first match as chairman of a club at Wembley Stadium. As I said when I was given that interesting piece of information: 'If that is so, then it is an all-time record that may some time be equalled but it can never be beaten.' What a start! Now with forty-two league matches to follow in 1988–9, plus cup matches, I had a lot of football ahead of me. I was not very impressed when I found out the poor attendances that supported the team.

It is not my intention to bore you by going through all the league matches. However, regarding the FA Cup it is the ambition of every non-league club to go through the qualifying rounds and then be entered in the first round proper with some football league clubs.

After getting that far, it is every non-league club's ambition to get through the first two rounds and in with the big clubs from the premier division and the football league, first division, with the possibility of a very rich 'pay day'. Well Hendon got in with the first lot of football league clubs by getting through all the qualifying rounds. Looking forward to the draw for the first round proper was very exciting. The match to be played on Saturday, 19 November 1988 was Reading v. Hendon at Elm Park, Reading. We achieved a good draw and had hopes that we might become giant-killers but it was not to be. It was a very exciting game but, in the end, Reading's league experience saw them through.

I enjoyed all the matches – home and away. Every match was special. As this first team's standard was higher than anything that I had been involved in previously, the involvement was really special. But I then had a health problem again. At this time I was still driving my car, but I wondered for how long. Early in 1990, I was at the home ground enjoying a match and wondering how long I would last. Then, just after half-time, I felt that I had better drive home. I did, very slowly, and when I got there I knew that it was unlikely, because of the way I felt, that I would be going to any more of Hendon's matches. So, common sense dictated the only possible course and I resigned as chairman. Since then, the only way I can follow the progress of Hendon is through the results and league tables in the Sunday papers.

Now my only positive way of being involved in football is by doing the pools every week. I go through the fixtures diligently and make my forecast. I think that I know the answers, until I see the results. But who knows? Maybe next week will be the time when I will have eight score draws on one line.

Football today is so different from the sport that I learned about. In those days any games that I played in were for enjoyment. Maybe I was wrong but for me money was never a motivating factor.

I I

MULTIPLE SCLEROSIS

I have given this matter a lot of consideration and decided that to tell my story it is necessary for me to begin with the position that I am now in at the age of seventy years plus. I was always fit and active, playing weekly five-a-side soccer and regular golf well into my forties. Then in mid-December 1978 something happened which was apparently unconnected with my own health. My eldest sister Mary, who had been suffering from cancer for some months, died on 17 December. She left a grieving husband and ten children, the youngest under two years old. My father, my three remaining sisters, Eileen, Patsy and Kathleen, my brother, John and I were very upset about her death and we wondered how we would cope. Anyway, I continued with my weekly golf and indoor football and did not appear to be any different from what I was before the tragedy.

At forty-three years of age I continued to play five-a-side soccer for my firm's team in a London business houses indoor league. On a Thursday some time in February 1979, we had our usual weekly match. Getting out of bed that morning I felt pins and needles in my right leg. Nothing extraordinary, I thought, but I had some difficulty in walking down the stairs to breakfast. My leg became numb but I thought it was just a passing thing. In fact it got worse and the numbness extended up to my chest. It was

145

really bothering me so I decided to withdraw from the football team. I was not feeling good and did not know what was going on. My right leg just did not get better but I still thought that it was no big deal. The pins and needles continued on and off over the next few weeks. I finally decided to go to the doctor and tell him what was happening.

I had known the doctor for a few years and after he finished examining me we had a long chat. He told me that he could not tell me immediately what was wrong and asked me to come back in a week and tell him how I was. Nothing had changed and when I told the doctor he told me what he thought and what he decided should be done. He told me that from the description of the symptoms I could be suffering from multiple sclerosis (MS). He also said that MS is a very strange disorder. It does not have any clear-cut symptoms in its early stages and it is very difficult to predict the likely course of the disease over a number of years. Problems experienced by one sufferer may be quite unlike those experienced by another. In my case all my right side was affected, which meant I had to start writing with my left hand. I had numbness, pins and needles a slight and temporary disturbance of vision and balance problems. I found that I was liable to trip over the corner of carpets or on uneven surfaces.

The doctor told me that he had decided to arrange for me to be admitted to the London Clinic for tests. I was finally called to the clinic on Tuesday 19 June 1979. The tests I went through included the most painful procedure I have ever had, lumbar puncture. Recovering from that was psychologically difficult, if only for a short time. Soon after that the neurologist came in to inform me that I was definitely suffering from MS. It is, I learned, a disease of regular relapses and remissions, which explained why I had some good days when I thought that there was nothing wrong with me and bad days when I thought the world had come to an end. On the good days my thoughts might go something like this: 'How could I have such a disease? I maintained a good standard of physical health and fitness all my life, having played over five hundred games of football, about a thousand games of golf (or maybe it just felt like that!) and a few seasons' table tennis. How could I have become disabled?

When I next met my doctor he first of all confirmed that his fears were right and then explained a few matters that I was not directly aware of. Although this disease has been around for many years, the medical profession have no idea about what causes it and, as a result, there is absolutely no cure for it. One of the nasty aspects of this disease, particularly in the early stages, is depression. Within the first few years I suffered from depression and I can state quite clearly that it is a very destructive illness. Only somebody who has suffered from this can speak about its misery. During that time it appeared that there was a big black cloud above my head and I seemed to shut out everybody. I took all sorts of pills and many more physical and emotional treatments but nothing appeared to change or cure me. I knew very little about MS, beyond having a vague recollection of seeing in some book at some time that it was a disabling disease and that people who suffer from it normally end up in a wheelchair. I couldn't imagine what the future might bring.

I decided to give up driving my car in the late 1980s. Common sense really made up my mind for me. I felt that if it was necessary to use one of my legs for the brake or accelerator and that leg could not move, an accident was inevitable. The reason I ceased to play golf was different. In 1987 it became just a good memory. It happened as follows: a golfing friend of mine, Matty Lennon, knew how much I liked golf. He occasionally took me to Crews Hill golf club, where he was a member, to play a few holes. It was obvious at the time that I could not play a full round. We went there on three occasions; on the first we played twelve holes and finished then because my difficulties would not allow me to play any more. Our second effort lasted just nine holes and we then returned to the clubhouse. The next one ended after just five holes. The first four holes did not produce any problems and I was getting around easily. The fifth was over water which was covered by a small bridge. On my way over I slipped and fell. I was taken back soaked to the clubhouse and after I had tidied myself up was brought home. That was my final effort on a golf course. What a way to finish!

I have come to terms with the fact that I cannot drive and have to rely on minicabs and friends to get around but I'm damned if I am going to throw in the towel completely. I can still hobble around with the aid of a Zimmer frame and the old Beatty bloody-mindedness tells me that I shall continue to do so until I am incapable of placing one foot in front of the other. Then, and only then, will I feel that MS has beaten me. Perhaps my dislike of wheelchairs is fuelled by the fact that I know they will become an inevitable part of my life one day. I am already forced to use them at airports and hospitals, where I accept them as a method of mobility, but I like to think that I will be keeping my feet on the ground for a few years to come. Where there is hope there is Beatty!

Realising that MS would not go away, I decided that a total contrast to the previous few years was needed. I have got that contrast mainly through my writing. I also retain my accountancy (registered auditor) practising certificate by attending the annual twenty-one hours of seminars on continuous professional development (CPD), and of course my faith is very important to me. This has made it an unequal challenge: I am winning. Yes, I am enjoying every moment of what I do.

A breakthrough on this disease may, the magazines say, take place 'soon', but after so many years of promises and disappointments I just cannot see it happening. Even if some cure is found it will take years of tests before it will be accepted

– certainly far too late for people like me. With all the lows in this, including the many relapses, it is, in my opinion, vital to create an alternative way of life. It is not easy. I am trying to and, hopefully, succeeding in putting the disease into the background and treating it in the same way as one treats the common cold.

As must have become clear I have done my share of organising charity golf events. The list of good causes that I have supported include the Oblate Fathers Missionary Fund and their training fund, the parish of Our Lady of Mount Carmel and St George, the Benburb Base, the Irish Chaplaincy in Britain and of course the Irish Centre. I made no distinction between the amounts of energy I devoted to each but I suppose, as a sufferer, I had a special interest in ARMS, the multiple sclerosis society.

I organised a one-off event at Trent Park Golf Club on 14 September 1983. A lot of people are involved in this society and the proceeds of the day were to help finance an innovation which, at the time, was produced to ease the symptoms of MS and make life more comfortable for some sufferers. It was a hyperbaric oxygen chamber which gave some people a lot of relief but did not help me. The MS charity was very happy with the proceeds of the day. It was my hope that somebody else would continue with it and make it an annual event.

As the message by Ronnie Lane of ARMS in the brochure for the day was so relevant to this disease, I decided to reproduce it here:

> Help us to wipe this terrible disease, multiple sclerosis, off the face of the earth! As with most things in life, money is one of the ingredients required. On the various fundraising functions organised to help purchase a hyperbaric oxygen chamber to help treat victims of the disease living in north London – and today's event is just one – the

main theme is 'Unity is Strength'! It is, for example, much easier to raise £100 by getting £1 from 100 people than by getting £100 from one person. My reason for dwelling on the money theme is quite simple – when the chamber is purchased a lot of money will be necessary to pay the running costs. Therefore, hopefully today's golf tournament will be an annual event.

Of course it must be stressed that this treatment is not a cure for the disease – unfortunately, there is no known cure – but, from the available evidence, it does help considerably in many cases. Hopefully, a cure will be found some day, but sooner rather than later. Now in 2006 the prospect of a permanent wheelchair is becoming closer, I feel more able to accept that fact now than if it had happened a few years ago. I no longer look back in anger to my days as a goal-scoring centre forward in my grade of football and as a middle-handicap golfer. Now I am able to look back over the programmes, paper cuttings and the memories and think how lucky I was and am. As I mentioned earlier, my main recreation is now writing, with my left hand (I no longer have the use of my right hand). Who knows: I may graduate eventually to writing a novel. It could be worse! On the plus side, I am so lucky to have a wonderful caring family. Life is good now and so long as my God allows me to continue, then here I am. One final point: I have always explained to my medical advisors that, in my opinion, MS started for me as a result of the shock to my nervous system when my sister Mary died. Medical opinion does not agree.

This maybe a good place to explain the part played by the Pioneer Total Abstinence Association in my life. It is necessary to go back to when it all started for me. I was confirmed on 28 May 1947 at Our Lady of Mount Carmel Church, in Kill, County Waterford, by the Most Rev Daniel Coholan DD, Bishop of

Waterford and Lismore. At the time all children who were confirmed took a pledge not to drink alcohol until their twenty-first birthday. I can still remember a comment at home at the time: 'I wonder how long it will last.' A short time later the association opened a branch in the local parish and sought members. I had never heard of that organisation before but when it was explained to me I joined as a probationer. At age sixteen years a full badge was available and of course I applied for and got it. The next big change was when I received the certificate and silver badge for twenty-five years membership. After the forty-year membership certificate I was now heading for the 'big one', the gold badge for fifty years membership. I was presented with that badge and certificate by Bishop Pat O'Donoghue at, appropriately, the celebratory function for my thirty-five years in practice as an accountant in London.

As a matter of policy I have always worn my badge and I have never at any time been tempted to taste or drink alcohol. It was just not my scene. Shortly after I started in business, I can remember a client advising me as follows: 'If you don't take down that pin and take a drink, you will not be in business for too long,' I remember also one Christmas many years ago making a delivery to a farm when I was a temporary postman. I was invited in for a drink. I thought it would be a cup of tea but no – a glass of whiskey was there 'for the postman'. I told them that I was a Pioneer. The farmer replied 'I am not interested. Since the 1920s every postman to this house had a glass of whiskey in Christmas week. You are no different.' He put his back against the front door. Only when I literally fought my way out did he realise that I would not do what he told me.

When I was secretary of a football club that played in a Sunday morning league one of my jobs was to pick up two players on my way to the ground. One of them was an excellent player when he was able but he had a drink problem. The first day I called for him his landlady told me that he was still in bed. He had had a late night and was in no fit state to play. One of our reserves took his place. Next Sunday it was the same story. I asked to see him. I woke him up and gave him an ultimatum: 'When you play you are one of our best players. But here in bed under the influence of alcohol, forget it. I will send you match details as usual but will not call again. You know that, without you, we are top of the league.' My ultimatum worked. The next week he was at our dressing room at the ground before anybody else. He told me that he had had no drink during the week and would miss no more matches. As good as his word, he never missed another match. We won the league and at our celebration I saw him with a glass of orange in his hand. We have since lost touch but I sometimes wondered if he stayed 'dry' after that and for how long!

I recently read a very touching article on the Pioneer prayer in a recent issue of *Pioneer*, the association's magazine. This led me to think of my own position as a lifelong member and I decided to put my thoughts in writing about what being a Pioneer means to me since I first took the pledge in May 1947. In those youthful days of membership I was very interested in sport and like most young lads at the time I hoped for stardom. I recall that my personal superstars at the time were the Waterford hurlers and the Irish soccer stars. I remember my father, God rest him, saying to me: 'If you want to get anywhere in sport never drink alcohol or smoke.' Although I had plenty of success at my own level in sport, I never got to the professional level at any sport. I was not good enough.

After so many years in practice as an accountant I still wear the Pioneer pin proudly. In the early years when I was invited on many occasions to various dinner dances and other functions it was normal to be offered a drink on arrival. Inevitably it would be some form of alcohol. In those days people were surprised when I requested a soft drink. People who know me are aware that I have no interest in alcohol and they respect my pin. Sometimes individuals try to be awkward and it is necessary to take a tough stance when saying 'No.'

From the time the *Irish Post* started in 1970 until we sold out to the Smurfit organisation in June 1986, I was the chairman. During that time, apart from still running my accountancy practice, I was very involved in the newspaper work – particularly in public relations. This, as readers will have already learned, involved official openings of clubs, presenting prizes, attending dinner dances and making speeches. At every function, without exception, alcohol was offered to me. But the message got through – eventually. On one occasion in the 1970s I was invited as a guest to a Pioneer annual dinner dance in Birmingham. That was very special. To myself (and to others) I have proved that it is not necessary to drink alcohol to be successful in business. Now, in the autumn of my life, I still wear the pin and, when necessary, I take great pride in explaining what it means. Of course, like all Pioneers, I accept my obligation to recite the Heroic Offering twice daily. That is now part of my life. What does it mean to me? Well, let's go through it:

> For Thy greater glory and consolation, O Sacred Heart of Jesus; for Thy sake to give good example, to practise self-denial, to make reparation to thee for the sins of intemperance and for the conversion of excessive drinkers, I will abstain for life from all spirituous drink.

The prayer says it all. In effect I am describing that I agree with the words and hope that my way of life helps somebody who has or had a drink problem. To conclude I can only say that I am very proud to be able to say: 'I am a Pioneer.'

I 2

FINALE

Qualifying in my profession is not easy. Some get there eventually. A lot do not. How I got where I am today is detailed earlier in this book. Each year a members' council is in charge of each accountancy body, to deal with all relevant professional matters. I was fortunate enough to have been elected a council member of the Institute of Certified Public Accounts in Ireland in the seventies and again on 29 March 1991. The latter appointment lasted until 1995 as I was reappointed in 1993. I had the honour of being the first ever overseas council member. With all the EU moves affecting accountants, this was a good time to have been a council member especially since the meetings took place in Ireland every few weeks.

Yes, I am justly proud of what I have achieved in the accountancy profession. Thankfully our family did very well in their student lives: Catherine got her degree in home economics at Surrey University, Claire graduated with a mathematics degree from Warwick and Ian got his degree in engineering at Bradford. All three got excellent jobs in their chosen professions. Catherine was the first to get married. She left her job and has three lovely children, Marianne, Elizabeth and Richard. Claire also got married and has three children – Megan, Siobhan and Eleanor.

As I said earlier, what I did in accountancy made me feel

very proud but it has paled into insignificance compared to what Catherine achieved. When her three children were settled in at school, she decided that she wanted to do something else. When she was making up her mind about what she would do she decided: 'My dad is an accountant, my husband is an accountant, so I will be one too!' What happened then was like a fairytale. She enrolled with the Chartered Association of Certified Accountants, took her first examination in June 1992 and qualified in December 1994. That was excellent, but soon after getting her results she got another letter from the association, informing her that she had won the silver medal for second place in the world. In addition, she had also been awarded the individual prize for Paper 12 for achieving the highest mark in this paper in the UK and Ireland. The prizes and medal were awarded at a presentation ceremony held at the association's head office in Lincoln's Inn Fields, London on the 10 April 1995. Breda and I went to the ceremony. It was wonderful.

But awards did not end there for Catherine. She was also awarded one of the *Irish Post*'s Irish Person of the Year awards for 1995. This presentation was made by His Excellency, Mr T. Barrington, the Irish ambassador. Because of a serious accident suffered by her husband, Peter, a few days before the presentation at the Grosvenor House Hotel in Park Lane, London, on 18 April 1996, she could not attend. Her brother, Ian, accepted the award on her behalf. Peter recovered and is now the practice manager at Beatty and Company. Catherine now works as a lecturer in accountancy and I'm still a registered auditor.

I would just like to add that Catherine's daughter, Marianne, our eldest granddaughter, won a place at Cambridge after attending Haberdashers School in Hertfordshire. Her subject was economics. Her family were very proud of her when she received her first-class honours degree in June 2004. She is now working with an eminent accountancy firm in London and studying to be

– yes, you've guessed it – an accountant! I have a lot to answer for!

Catherine's second daughter, Elizabeth, also won a place at Cambridge and is reading natural sciences. Elizabeth is still a member of St Catherine's Choir at Haberdashers. Last year (2005) she was part of the choir that took part in the Youth's National Competition for Choirs. Her choir came first and it was great to hear them on the radio and see them performing their winning songs on television. A proud moment for all the family.

To see the joy of our grandchildren with Breda these days is beautiful and special.

ACKNOWLEDGEMENTS

I would like to thank the following family members who were helpful in providing me with information and in so many other ways:

My sister, Patsy Carey, who typed this book, and her husband Denis who ferried the manuscripts to and from my house.

Eileen Lonergan, my sister, and her husband Matt. They always made me welcome in their house and looked after me so well on my trips to Ireland.

My brother, John Beatty of Abbeyside, Dungarvan. We always enjoy a day touring the south-east when I go Ireland on a visit.

My younger sister Kathleen (Kally) now lives in Scotland with her husband John. She travelled from her home to look after me on several occasions.

My cousin Margaret Coleman (neé Beatty), who still lives in Abbeyside, Dungarvan. My father was born in Abbeyside.

Aileen Kiely, Dungarvan, my first cousin.

I would also like to thank the following friends and acquaintances who provided me with information:

Roy Battye, Kilmacthomas

Father Jim Butler, OMI whose help with my charity work for the Irish Centre, Camden Town I really appreciated. He comes from County Leitrim and now lives in Dublin.

Jim Conway, professional footballer with Fulham, Manchester City, Ireland and then Portland Timbers, Oregan. USA. He it was who agreed with me to bring the famous footballers to Kilmacthomas in 1976, 1977 and 1978.

Jerry Daly, London and Kerry, friend and proofreader.

John Devine, professional footballer with Arsenal, Norwich City and Ireland: the last of the stars who travelled to Kilmacthomas in June 1978.

Father Bobby Gilmore. During his years as head of the Irish Chaplaincy in Britain I did some charity work for him and he was a great supporter and help to me in the other charity work I carried out.

Danny Kirwan, publican, Kilmacthomas, County Waterford. I spent many hours in his shop in the mid- and late-1940s discussing sport with his late father Percy Kirwan.

Father Ken McCabe. I carried out some fundraising for the Lillie Road Centre, of which he was head. He was very helpful to me when I had the idea of writing this book.

Frank Murphy, editor of the *Irish Post*

Seamus O'Brien, Abbeyside, Dungarvan

Bob Phelan, Waterford.

Sr Teresa, Convent of Mercy, Kilmacthomas (now closed). She now lives in Dungarvan.

Sean Ryan, Dublin

Michael Thornhill, London and Limerick, friend and proofreader

Ed Wymberry, Waterford

John Young, writer, Abbeyside, Dungarvan

I also wish to acknowledge information received from the Guildhall Library in London about the ship that my Uncle Jack worked on during the war years.

Finally I want to thank my wife, my children and my grandchildren for being there.